150

MICHAEL & CAROLINE CARROLL

TYNDALE
KIDS

TYNDALE HOUSE PUBLISHERS, INC.
WHEATON, ILLINOIS

Edited by Betty Free

Designed by Jackie Noe

Published in association with the literary agency of Alive Communications, Inc., 7680 Goddard Street, Suite 200, Colorado Springs, CO 80920.

Library of Congress Cataloging-in-Publication Data

Carroll, Michael W., date
  Absolutely awesome : the things God has made / Michael and Caroline Carroll.
    p.   cm.
  Includes bibliographical references and indexes.
  Summary: A collection of devotional readings combining facts about nature with spiritual truths from the Bible and expressing the wonders of creation as they apply to contemporary life.
  ISBN 0-8423-3043-7 (pbk.)
  1. Creation Juvenile literature.   2. Nature—Religious aspects—Christianity Juvenile literature.   3. Human ecology—Religious aspects—Christianity juvenile literature.   [1. Creation.   2. Nature—Religious aspects—Chrstianity.   3. Christian life.   4. Prayer books and devotions.]   I. Carroll, Caroline, date.
  II. Title.
BT695.C335   1999
231.7'65—dc21   99-31845

Printed in Singapore

06 05 04 03 02 01 00
8   7   6   5   4   3   2

To our children, Andy and Allie

From the time the world was created, people have
seen the earth and sky and all that God made.
They can clearly see his invisible qualities—
his eternal power and divine nature.

ROMANS 1:20

CONTENTS

ACKNOWLEDGMENTS

The authors wish to thank the following science reviewers. While not specifically endorsing this book, they didn't throw anything at us, and they seemed to think our science was all right. We are grateful for their time and contributions toward making this the spectacular, wonderful, fun, and mostly fabulous book we hope it is! They are, in order of their chapters:

Scott Elias, fellow of the Institute for Arctic and Alpine Research

James McAdams, planetary scientist at Johns Hopkins University's Applied Physics Laboratory

Jack Murphy, geologist at the Denver Museum of Natural History

Matthew Golombeck, principal investigator for Mars Pathfinder

Paula Cushing, curator of entomology and arachnology at the Denver Museum of Natural History

Anil Rao, associate professor of biology at Metro State College, Denver, Colorado

Kirk Johnson, curator of paleobotany at the Denver Museum of Natural History

William K. Hartmann, senior scientist at the Planetary Science Institute

Dave Head, climatologist, Bureau of Indian Affairs

Diana Wiggam, interpretive ranger at Rocky Mountain National Park

Hugh Ross, astrophysicist, founder of Reasons to Believe

Also, Karen Watson, Betty Free, Beth Sparkman, and Jackie Noe of Tyndale House Publishers for making us look good; Jeff Tikson, who believed we could actually do this; Mickie Cain (we picked your brain—hope it doesn't start to rain!); David Grinspoon, "rock weatherman"; Bill "through-the-lens" Gerrish; and the many others whose labors and prayers served to make this book a tool for the kingdom.

GOD'S
fingerprints

These are some of the minor things he does, merely a whisper of his power. Who can understand the thunder of his power?

JOB 26:14

The shape of giant spiral galaxies, hurricanes, and tiny sea shells all echo a pattern that God has put upon the universe.

DAY 1: CHAOS-FREE CREATION

Hurricane Emilia wheels across the Pacific ocean, looking like other spirals in nature—the big and the small. (Photo courtesy NASA/JSC.)

Emptiness, formlessness, darkness. Nothingness—no order—chaos. Then there *is* something. It is light! The sky appears, then land and seas. Plants and trees fill the land; a sun, a moon, and stars fill the sky. Fish and other sea creatures fill the water; birds fill the sky; animals appear on the land. Finally, people fill the earth and take charge of it. God brings order.

There is nothing disorganized about the way the universe has been put together. From a little spiral seashell to the most outrageous galaxy, we see patterns in the stuff of nature.

The pinwheel cloud formations of hurricanes remind us of spiral galaxies scattered across the universe. We see the same pattern "spinnin' " through the shell of the chambered nautilus and even in the water that swirls down our bathtub drain. And check this out: The cloud of gigantic comets, asteroids, and planets in our solar system is a lot like a tiny atom, with its orbiting electrons huddled around a starlike center. Nature repeats patterns over and over, big and small.

God leaves echoes of patterns in the waves of pools, the winds of hurricanes, and the spiral of stars to show us his organization. We will learn more about these patterns in the days ahead.

As an artist signs his works of art, so God uses patterns for his signature, signing his work for us to see. Out of chaos he has brought order, and the universe pulses with the beat of his extreme creativity.

Think about what God says to you

> *For God is not a God of disorder but of peace.*
> I CORINTHIANS 14:33

One reason why learning about science is so much fun is that it can help us discover new things about God. Through science we can become aware of the orderly patterns God has used in all that he has made. Everything in the universe, from the biggest star to the smallest atom, from the cycle of the seasons to the workings of our human bodies, has God's fingerprints on it. God wants us to look around us and see him.

Let's talk to God!

MY JOURNAL (choose one)

God, sometimes my life feels like chaos! Here are some things that I need you to help me make sense out of:

_____

_____

_____

_____

Lord, this is a place where I see your order in my world:

_____

_____

_____

_____

Your orderliness gives me peace because:

_____

_____

_____

_____

MY PRAYER

Thank you, God, for showing yourself in the spirals of galaxies, the pinwheels of hurricanes, and every other awesome pattern you've created. Help me to see you in everything around me. I'm glad you give my life peacefulness and order!

Atoms make up everything, including:

- the ink that forms the words on this page
- the paper that these words are printed on
- the eyes that you are reading with
- the brain that you are hopefully thinking with
- the air that you are breathing
- even the chair, couch, floor, or bed that you are sitting on

Atoms are the cosmic building blocks of the universe—God's Tinkertoy set. And they're tiny to the extreme. The period at the end of the last sentence has about 250,000 million atoms! (Makes a man-made microchip seem like an elephant, huh?) Some atoms are smaller than others, depending on what they make up. The smaller the atom, the less it weighs. Hydrogen atoms are the lightest. Metals like uranium are the heaviest. (Gas is light, metal is heavy, see? This stuff's not so hard!)

There is a structure even to dinky little atoms. They have a center called a *nucleus*. The nucleus of hydrogen is made of one *proton,* and around it twirls one *electron.* Simple? Yep, but an atom of carbon has six protons in the middle, and six other things called *neutrons,* and all around that package spin six more electrons! Wow!

But wait—there's more! Protons, neutrons, and electrons are made

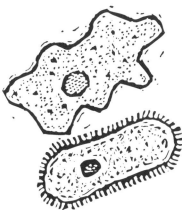

of even smaller things called *quarks.* Where will it all end?

Within atoms we find a force that holds everything together. It's called the strong nuclear force. What's really cool is that if the strong nuclear force were any stronger, hydrogen would be rare in the universe because it would stick to itself and make heavier things, such as iron. There would be no light stuff, such as the oxygen we need to breathe. But if the strong nuclear force were weaker, just about everything would still be hydrogen, which is what God used to start the universe. There would be nothing heavy to build planets with, no minerals for rocks, and no calcium for bones. In other words, we wouldn't be here!

God has made the strong nuclear force—the "glue" of the universe—just powerful enough for life. That's no coincidence—not even close. And the tiny electrons whirling around their nucleus are a lot like our planets zooming around the sun. The structure of these things leaves no doubt: God is here! Nature's tiny structures and strong forces tell us of a guiding force, a Master Architect.

Think about what God says to you

> *He existed before everything else began,*
> *and he holds all creation together.*
> *Colossians 1:17*

God set up the strong nuclear force to hold the universe together long before we were here, and he controls our universe in ways we can't even imagine.

Let's talk to God!

MY JOURNAL (choose one)

Thank you, God, for the following friends and relatives—people whom you have put in my life to help me hold things together:

_____

_____

_____

_____

_____

Here is an area of my life where I feel as if things are coming apart and I need more of your "glue":

_____

_____

_____

_____

MY PRAYER

Lord, your wondrous design of nature around me is proof positive of a loving Creator. Help me always remember to let you be the one who holds my life together.

There are some really, really big things in our world. Mount Everest is so tall that the sky above it is black. It's as high as airliners fly. There are even taller mountains on other planets (see Week 4). People have built some big things too. The tallest buildings in the world are over fifteen

Betelgeuse is a gigantic star that could hold 268 million suns. This painting shows what it might look like.

hundred feet tall (ninety-five floors), and the largest building in the world is the Vehicle Assembly Building at Cape Kennedy, where they put space shuttles together. It is such a mega-building that it actually has its own weather inside!

Some of the coolest big things are creatures that run, dive, jump, and swim around. Blue Whales are as heavy as fifteen elephants, and giant sequoia trees are heavier than fourteen Blue Whales—twenty-one hundred tons. (That's like fifteen hundred cars!) Some sequoia trees grow as tall as a thirty-five-story skyscraper.

Really big trees like this Giant Sequoia in California can grow as tall as a thirty-five-floor skyscraper.

The most famous big beasties of the past were the dinosaurs. They were some of the tallest, meanest, fastest, fiercest things that ever stomped the dirt. *Tyrannosaurus rex* had teeth five inches long. And speaking of long, some apatosaurs may have been one hundred feet long from nose to tail.

The Vehicle Assembly Building, where space shuttles are put together, is the largest enclosed space on Earth. (Photo courtesy NASA Arts Program)

Farther out in space there are things much bigger than our minds can imagine. The sun can hold one million earths inside of it. You think that's big? Try this one: The star Betelgeuse is a red giant that can hold 268 million of our own suns—awesome! The weird thing is that the bigger a star starts out, the shorter its life will be. Stars that are a lot bigger than the sun will blow themselves up. (Ah, the life of a star.)

Big stars blow up. Big dinosaurs have died out. Big is not always best, no matter what anybody says. Even the tallest mountains that God made won't last—they will eventually wear away. Thank God that he is bigger than anything else, and he will last forever.

Think about what God says to you

> *He counts the stars and calls them all by name.*
> *How great is our Lord! His power is absolute!*
> PSALM 147:4-5

When we lose sight of how big and powerful God is, two things can happen:

1. We'll try to be "big" and be our own god.
2. We'll start to feel stressed out and overwhelmed as we try to cope with life without going to God for strength and help.

Let's talk to God!

MY JOURNAL (choose one)

Here is an area of my life in which I struggle with wanting to be bigger and more important:

_____

_____

_____

_____

Here is something that feels like a really big deal in my life that I want you to help me handle:

_____

_____

_____

_____

MY PRAYER

God, you are the biggest there is—bigger than anything you have made. You put huge things on this earth to help me remember that. Thank you for being bigger than any problem I will ever face. And help me not to get too big for my britches!

At first you might think a small daisy and a large palm tree don't have much in common. But take a closer look at the petals of a daisy, the trunk of a palm, and even the plates of a pinecone or the face of a sunflower. You'll see a repeat pattern in the turn of each spiral that's mathematically exact. No, really. It's the same for the tiniest pinecone and the tallest palm tree.

All of these plants, and many others, follow a mysterious formula in which each number of turns follows a pattern. But you don't have to be a rocket scientist to figure it out. You can find this spiral pattern by counting. (Don't count on your fingers, though—you'll run out.) As you count, add the last two numbers to get your next one. So what do you get? One, two, three, five, eight, thirteen, twenty-one, and so on.

Now look at the head of a sunflower. There are two spirals. One goes clockwise, the other goes counterclockwise. If you count the spirals in each direction, they follow our counting pattern. (Sunflower spirals have thirteen one way and twenty-one the other, or thirty-four one way and fifty-five the other. Should we keep counting?) The same thing happens with the twin spirals of pinecone scales and the "eyes" of pineapples, which form three spirals. We see this pattern in plants all over the world. It's just another place where God shows us his organization. We see his order in the patterns of his veggies!

(Think it's confusing? Don't sweat it; so do people who study plants.) What a wonderful mind God has, to have thought up all these neat designs.

God always has a pattern and a plan, and his plan is perfect. He loves you and has a special plan for you, too. Look for the patterns in your life to see if you can use them for clues about what God has planned for you. Do you love pets and have lots of them? Maybe you will grow up to be a veterinarian and help take care of God's creatures. Do you find yourself fascinated with faraway places and the people who live there? Maybe you will be a missionary to a foreign country. Is your neighborhood full of friends who don't know God? Perhaps God plans for you to share his Good News with them.

Think about what God says to you

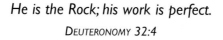

He is the Rock; his work is perfect.
DEUTERONOMY 32:4

God's designs and patterns show us his perfection.

Let's talk to God!

MY JOURNAL (choose one)
A pattern in my life that I appreciate as a gift from God is:

_____

_____

_____

_____

I see a pattern in my life, and this is how God might want me to use it right now:

_____

_____

_____

_____

Here is a way that God might want me to use this pattern when I grow up:

_____

_____

_____

_____

MY PRAYER

God, thank you for the design you have for my life. Sometimes when I'm in the middle of things, I can't see your plan or your pattern, and I wonder what in the world you are doing! But later (sometimes a lot later!) I can look back and see the pattern and understand more clearly what your goal is for me.

DAY 5: Branches in the Trees

God's fingerprint is on everything. One pattern we see, big and small, is called *dendritic*. Sound like something that's gone extinct? Dendritic means "branching," and nature just branches out all over. Look around!

The branches of a tree begin at the thick trunk, then spread out with thinner and thinner arms until the ends become teensy twigs. This branching pattern is found in your own body. Blood vessels are like tree trunks. As they spread out from your heart, they become smaller veins and arteries, and finally thin capillaries. (The next time you go for a drive, watch for even more dendritic stuff. Highways branch into country roads. Rivers branch out into small streams as they flow across the landscape. You can always count on the thin sticks, veins, streams, or highways to lead back to the big ones. They'll finally get back to the source—the roots, the heart, the lake, the city.) Cool design. Don't you wish you'd thought of it?

God's Son, Jesus, calls himself "the vine." We're like little branches, and God finds many ways to bring us to Jesus, our source. Sometimes God sends a friend to encourage us. Sometimes he talks to us through a book—and always through the Bible. Maybe a crisis in our life drives us to him, or the sight of a "way cool" sunset or thundering waterfall gets us excited about God's creative power. Whatever it takes, God wants to lead us back to his Son. Jesus wants to be our source, even when we're wandering branches trying to cut ourselves off from him. He loves us that much. It's a radical kind of love that doesn't care where we come from or how much we have blown it. That's real love—amazing love.

The branching form of dribbles in the sand is also found in trees, highway systems, and even in your body!

Think about what God says to you

> Remain in me, and I will remain in you. For a branch cannot produce fruit if it is severed from the vine, and you cannot be fruitful apart from me. Yes, I am the vine; you are the branches. Those who remain in me, and I in them, will produce much fruit. For apart from me you can do nothing.
>
> JOHN 15:4-5

When a stream is cut off from a river, it dries up. When a branch is cut off a tree, it stops bearing fruit. What happens when we are cut off from God? Nothing good, right? Stay connected. As Jesus says, "Remain in me."

Let's talk to God!

MY JOURNAL (choose one)

These are some ways that I can be more connected to God through his Son, Jesus:

_____

_____

_____

_____

These are some things in my life that have been cutting me off from God:

_____

_____

_____

_____

MY PRAYER

God, help me to stay connected to you as my source of power in the day-to-day grind. Through your Son, Jesus, you give me strength when I don't feel strong. You give me peace and joy, too, as I receive power to do the things that please you.

Activity Ideas for Week 1

1. Mega- and Mini-Mystery Montage:

Take a look at these mystery photos. Can you guess what all the spiral shapes are? The answers are upside down underneath the photos.

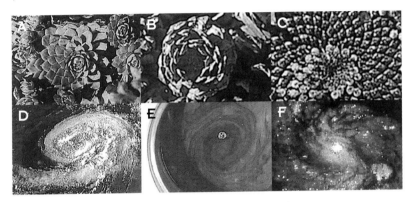

answers: A. houseleek plant   B. pinecone   C. sunflower   D. hurricane Bonnie   E. milk in coffee   F. spiral galaxy

2. Branching Out

Go outdoors to your backyard or to a playground, and build yourself a mini-mountain with a pile of dirt or sand. Now slowly pour a pitcher of water over the top of it and watch how the "rivers" branch into smaller streams as they flow downhill.

3. Invisible Forces

Put a table knife on the floor, and place a refrigerator magnet on it. Gravity holds the knife on the ground, but what happens when you pick up the magnet? Which force is stronger, gravity or electro-magnetism?

HOME
sweet home

Then God said to Noah, "Yes, this is the sign of my covenant with all the creatures of the earth."

GENESIS 9:17

Our world is sheltered from space by a blanket of air, ozone, and other protective layers. (Painting by Michael Carroll originally published in The New Star, a Tamarind Book by SU Publishing, Bedfordshire, England, 1997)

Our world is totally different from any other planet. As Dr. Frankenstein said, "It's ALIVE!!!" Compared to all the desolate planets we have seen up close, ours is an oasis of life floating through space. It seems that God designed this world just so that life could crawl all over it. It is warm enough for liquid water, which you can find in places like the ocean, rivers, and toilet bowls. And it's cool enough that things don't cook (unless you are a restaurant chef, and that's what you do).

Our two next-door planets are great examples of desolation. Venus, which is a little closer to the sun than Earth, is so hot that water boils away into the poisonous sky. It rains, but the rain is sulfuric acid. A nice summer evening checks in at about nine hundred degrees Fahrenheit, so don't bring any sunglasses—they will just melt. Our other cosmic neighbor is Mars, slightly farther from the sun than we are. It's too cold there for liquid water. Even if there were any puddles, they would boil instantly, not because of heat but because there is so little air to keep water liquid. Like an old song says, "Mars ain't the kind of place to raise your kids." Venus is too hot, and Mars is too cold; but like Goldilocks's porridge, Earth is just right.

Our home is just right for other reasons too.

- Our earth with its sun is exactly the right distance from the center of the Milky Way galaxy. If we were any closer, radiation from closely packed stars would fry us, and there would be no such thing as Milky Way candy bars.
- Speaking of the sun, Earth travels around the sun in a nearly circular orbit. If the orbit were more egg-shaped, our seasons would be too extreme for life. Summer would boil us, and winter would freeze us.
- Our moon is just the right size and distance from us to stir up the core of the earth, which creates a magnetic field. That magnetic field protects us from the sun's radiation.
- Even Jupiter gets into the act: This supermagnificent planet is so big that its strong gravity shields the earth from incoming meteors and comets. Jupiter pulls some of them into itself but throws most of them back into the outer solar system, where they won't bother Earth anymore.
- Most of the comets and meteors that get past Jupiter are burned up by our just-right atmosphere.

It's good that God thought of all this. Space—it's a jungle out there!

Think about what God says to you

> Let all who take refuge in you rejoice; let them sing joyful praises forever. Protect them, so all who love your name may be filled with joy.
>
> PSALM 5: 11

We have seen how God has protected our home in space from deadly meteors, radiation, heat, and cold. He is even more interested in protecting people. He spreads his protection over us. As the psalmist says, God wants us to find joy in his protection.

Let's talk to God!

MY JOURNAL (choose one)

One time that God protected me was when:

_____

_____

_____

_____

Here is an area where I feel I need God's extra protection:

_____

_____

_____

_____

MY PRAYER

Thank you, Lord, for giving me a safe place to live. Thanks, too, for guarding me against things in life that can hurt me or bring me down. When bad things happen, I know I can go to you, and you will encourage me.

DAY 2: PUZZLE PLANET

Planet Earth is weird—really, it's true. There are lots of planets with ice, clouds, rocks, sand, storms, sandstorms, nights, days, and seasons. The three worlds most like ours are covered with a crust (the yummiest part) made of rock a lot like Earth's. But there is no other planet that has a puzzle crust quite like ours.

Space shuttle astronauts took this photo of the Middle East, which clearly shows how the Sinai peninsula fits together with Egypt to the left, Israel and Saudi Arabia to the right. (Photo courtesy Johnson Space Center)

Our planet is split up like a gigantic drifting jigsaw puzzle. These puzzle pieces are called *tectonic plates*. They float on liquid rock inside the earth. There are chains of volcanoes along the edges of plates where one plate slides under another. Some of the plates bump into each other and push up mountains. Other tectonic plates pull away from each other. In places like Iceland, if you are very patient, you can watch the ground grow apart as fast as your fingernails grow. Still other plates grind together and make earthquakes. Earth is being bent, folded, and mutilated.

Bet you never knew what fast movers rocks are. Under our feet, as we speak, there is rock weather. Forty miles beneath the ground, some plates

This photo from the Jupiter-bound Galileo probe shows Africa. Saudi Arabia—at the right—has broken away from the African continent because of the world's drifting plates. (Photo courtesy NASA/JPL.)

that slip under others are forced deep into the hot earth. Layers of rock, like stone clouds, float in the red-hot goo until they melt. As they do, liquid rock is pushed up—a kind of rainstorm in reverse. Sometimes the lava (liquid rock) even rains onto the surface, where the underground rock weather meets the weather of the sky in the form of a volcano. Two kinds of weather. (Wonder if it's going to rock today.)

There's a reason for this rock

At Thingvellir in Iceland, two plates are pulling apart about three centimeters every century.

concert. When it rains (water, that is) all over the place, the good minerals in the soil get washed into the ocean. After enough time, if these minerals are never replaced, there will be no minerals left for plants, so no plants will grow for us. The world will be boring and dead. But what really happens is that the minerals end up at the bottom of the ocean, where the rock gets recycled. The rock gets pushed up by plates and made into high ground again.

While all this is going on, the rocks are changing. When the lava that spurts out of volcanoes becomes hard rock, it's called *igneous*. Igneous rock gets broken down into sand and dust, and these get stuck together in layers, magically turning into sedimentary rock. Some sedimentary rock, like limestone, is made up of dead animals and plants. If igneous or sedimentary rock is under enough pressure (and we've all felt that), it becomes metamorphic or "changed" rock. Soft limestone, for example, becomes hard marble if it is really squished. Eventually these rocks are lifted up into the highest mountains by the force of Earth's tectonic plates.

As Christians, we know that there is a reason for everything that happens to us. Sometimes, though, when life gets hard and we are under pressure, it doesn't feel so good. Then it's easy to forget that God is in control and will use the tough times for our good. God lifts us up, just as he has lifted up the mountains. And like the limestone that turns into beautiful marble, God is transforming us into something more beautiful with each experience in life. Through the good and the bad, he is making us more like Christ.

Think about what God says to you

So humble yourselves under the mighty power of God, and in his good time he will honor you. Give all your worries and cares to God, for he cares about what happens to you.

1 PETER 5: 6-7

Often the Bible talks about how God will lift us up and honor us. The Lord of the universe wants us to live full, spectacular lives "to the max." So when we are going through bad times and feel as if we're being squished, we need to remember that we can tell God how we feel. We can let him take care of us, because he does care.

Let's talk to God!

MY JOURNAL (choose one)

This is an area of my life where I can feel you putting pressure on me to change and grow:

_____

_____

_____

Lord, this is something I really worry about:

_____

_____

MY PRAYER

Lord, the way you have designed the pieces of our puzzle world so that we could live here is absolutely awesome. In the hard times, help me to remember that you will lift me up and make me into someone who is more like your Son, Jesus.

Cardboard Tectonics

This is a fun way to see how the earth's tectonic plates move. Cut a piece of heavy poster board or cardboard (the earth's crust) into four pieces. Gently place them in a large pan of warm water (liquid rock) with their sides close together. Add a drop or two of dishwashing liquid (erupting lava) to the water right where the cardboard pieces meet. Voilà—plate tectonics!

This volcano in Hawaii is helping to recycle Earth's atmosphere. (Photo courtesy William K. Hartmann)

Carbon dioxide is poisonous to most animal life, but that's OK because here on Earth, plants breathe carbon dioxide in and oxygen out. On the other hand, some of your best friends undoubtedly breathe in oxygen and breathe out carbon dioxide, so it's a pretty good trade between plants and animals. The swap has been happening for quite some time.

Both Venus and Mars have atmospheres of mostly carbon dioxide. So here is a good question: If God used the same building blocks for all the planets, what happened to all of Earth's carbon dioxide? Why are we able to breathe the air here but would not be able to do so on Mars or Venus?

Believe it or not, it's really our rocks that provide our nice, fresh air—yep, rocks. Earth does something that no other planet in the solar system does, and this is how it works: Carbon dioxide in the air combines with water in the form of snow, rain, hail—you name it. The rain falls down and runs all over the rocks. The water washes the carbon dioxide, along with other gases, into the rocks. If this goes on long enough, there won't be much air left, but don't start holding your breath yet.

God designed our planet to recycle this stuff from the rocks back into the air. The rocks ram into each other at the edge of those tectonic plates we talked about yesterday. This makes the rocks melt; and when they do, all the trapped gas has to get out in some way. (If you ever ate beans, you know all about this.) The gas gets out through the volcanoes, and presto, new air!

What would happen if we didn't have a recycling planet? Take a look at Mars—almost no air. It has lots of big volcanoes, but they're all dead or at least asleep. As oxygen-breathing creatures, we want to know: Where did the oxygen go? Martian rocks are red, and that's a clue. When an old nail rusts, it takes in oxygen and turns red. (Maybe it's embarrassed, who knows?) Most of the oxygen on Mars—and lots of the rest of its air—is locked in the rocks. The rocks are red because they have rusted, more or less, sucking in the oxygen. The thin leftovers are mostly carbon dioxide. The rocks don't move on Mars, the volcanoes don't go anymore, and presto, no air!

Venus is another planet with no recycling plan. On Earth, we have oceans that help to make limestone. Limestone sucks up the extra carbon dioxide, so Earth doesn't have too much. Venus's air doesn't get sucked into its rocks, and it has more carbon dioxide and a much hotter atmosphere than Mars. Its blanket of air is a hellish nine hundred-degree furnace of dense carbon dioxide. If you're a plant, there's lots to breathe there, but you'll be instant charcoal.

It's pretty cool how God designed our world so that it uses rocks as air fresheners. If plants could talk, they'd say it's cool too. We see God's recycling plan in many things around us, from the rains to the rocks.

God's message to us is like that. His words will always make a difference in our lives, and the Spirit of God will blow through our core like fresh air.

Think about what God says to you

Great is his faithfulness; his mercies begin afresh each day.
LAMENTATIONS 3:23

God has always been faithful and will be for all eternity. He just asks us to trust him each day, one day at a time. And he gives us new blessings every day. Learning to trust God in the little things today helps us to trust him for big things in the future, too.

Let's talk to God!

MY JOURNAL (choose one)

Here is an area of my life that is a little stinky right now—I need some of your Spirit's air freshener:

_____

_____

_____

_____

Here is a way that you have been faithful to me over and over again, and I want to thank you for it:

_____

_____

_____

_____

MY PRAYER

Lord, just as you make the air fresh and clean for me to breathe, you make my life fresh and new each day. Thank you that every morning I wake up to a brand-new day with no mistakes in it—yet!

The ocean cools our days, warms our nights, and pumps lots of oxygen into our air.

From space, Earth looks different from any other place. The reason is that much of it is covered with water. Almost three-fourths of it, to be exact. That's a whole lot of water. Most of this water is sea water. In fact, if you could fill ten gigantic bathtubs with all the water from our lakes, streams, rivers, ponds, puddles, seas, and oceans, nine and a half of them would be filled with sea water.

If you want to send a Martian a postcard showing a typical scene on Earth, send him one of the ocean, for oceans are definitely where it's at. There are four oceans on Earth: Arctic, Indian, Atlantic, and Pacific. The Pacific is by far the largest and deepest. Its Mariana Trench is thirty-six thousand feet deep, which is as far below sea level as the distance airliners fly above sea level.

Oceans are more than just big blobs of water. They also even out the temperature so that our nights are not too cold and our days are not too hot. Without oceans we'd be cooking and freezing like the moon next door, where daytime temps get up to two hundred degrees Fahrenheit and nighttime chills fall to minus two hundred degrees.

It's nice to have an ocean around. Most of our planet's living things hang out in the water, from tiny plankton (fish food that makes most of our oxygen) to those colossal and "way cool" cetaceans, the whales.

People used to think the oceans were silent and dark in the depths. As it turns out, Davy Jones's locker (the bottom of the ocean) is a restless place. Massive currents send water flowing for hundreds or even thousands of miles, carrying fish and fish food from one sea to another, feeding the life of the oceans, and stirring up cool water with warm. A great wheel of water churns around the Atlantic from Florida up to the coast of Canada, across to Europe, down along Africa, and back to Florida. Part of this current is the Gulf Stream, an undersea river that helps ships to cross the ocean. Another current, El Niño, is a major "heat wave" of warm water that spreads across the ocean and affects the weather all over the world. Currents are difficult to see. But in 1990 when a ship full of sneakers sank in the North Pacific, scientists got a break and were able to track floating Nikes. (They just did it.)

With all this water on our planet, is it any wonder that the Bible often uses the phrase "living water"? These words describe the new life Christ gives us, helping us understand how the Holy Spirit fills us up and refreshes us. Water brings life. We wouldn't last many days if we didn't have fresh water to drink. In the same way, we wouldn't survive long at all in this bumpy world without the hope and strength the Holy Spirit gives us.

Think about what God says to you

If you believe in me, come and drink!
For the Scriptures declare that rivers of living water
will flow out from within.
JOHN 7:38

The Holy Spirit is our living water and our source of new life and hope.

Let's talk to God!

MY JOURNAL (choose one)

Here is something that I feel very hopeful and excited about:

_____

_____

_____

_____

Here is something I've been waiting a long time for, and I don't feel very hopeful anymore. Please give me a fresh "drink" of hope:

_____

_____

_____

_____

MY PRAYER

Thank you for always being able to give me a boost of hope and encouragement when the "currents" of my life seem to be taking me somewhere new and kind of scary.

Riddles from Davy Jones's Locker

Q: What is the deepest part of the Atlantic Ocean?
A: The bottom!

Q: Why couldn't the octopus tell her twins apart?
A: They were i-tentacle twins.

Q: Who do the fish call to fix the piano?
A: The piano tuna.

DAY 5: THE GREATEST WONDER ON EARTH

We've taken a look at many excellent things that make Earth special, but there is one we haven't mentioned yet. It sets our planet apart more than rocks or water or volcanoes, and it's the most important to God. We're talking about you—and the rest of the people that God has put here.

You do have company, of course. God has put an immensely diverse bunch of living things around you. Forests of towering redwoods and desert oases with swaying palm trees provide natural beauty, as well as homes for many of God's creatures. Lions and tigers and bears ("oh, my!") roam jungle and forest. There are bizarre and beautiful insects with lots of legs and graceful wings. There are wild birds with wilder colors: parrots, flamingos, magpies, and robins. Humongous elephants and hippos stomp through jungles, and microscopic googly-eyed spiders tiptoe along beaches. Beyond the beaches even more unusual living things exist: brightly colored anemones that look as if they wandered out of someone's garden and got lost in the tide pools; sea horses, sea stars, and sea cucumbers; sailfish and tuna. (Always remember: You cannot tune a fish.)

When God created this special planet, he put many marvelous forms of life on it. But his ultimate creation was human beings. As one of those humans, you are set apart. God gave you a mind to figure things out and a responsibility to care for this world. And

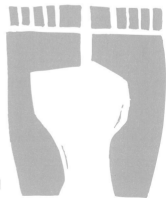

he gave you a soul. That's the spiritual, forever part of you that lives within your physical body.

Things as stupendous as Earth's magnetic fields are not what interest God most; it's the soul of each of his children, including you. When you die, it's not all over. There is a world beyond this one, and God wants you to enjoy it with him. He's set you apart to do his work, to share his joy, and to enjoy his creation.

Think about what God says to you

> *I will be your Father, and you will be my sons and daughters, says the Lord Almighty.*
> 2 CORINTHIANS 6:18

Christianity is the only religion in the world that is much more about a relationship between the Creator (that's God) and the created (that's you) than it is about all kinds of rules. It is the only religion in which the Creator has reached down and invited the created to become part of his own family.

Let's talk to God!

MY JOURNAL (choose one)

This is one reason I'm glad I'm your child:

_____

_____

_____

_____

This is something I'm going to ask you about when I'm with you in heaven: _____

_____

_____

_____

_____

MY PRAYER

Thank you for loving me enough to call me your child. Thank you for providing this world for me now and planning for me to spend forever with you in heaven. It will be awesome!

Ship Captains of the Bible

Cap'n Crunch may have great cereal, but there have been many ship captains before him.

Jonah tried to run away from God on a ship bound for Tarshish, but a storm overtook the ship he was on. When the crew realized that God had sent the storm because of Jonah, the ship's captain agreed to throw Jonah overboard (Jonah 1:3-15).

Many of the disciples were captains of their own fishing boats. Peter, Andrew, James, and John were all fishermen, and they had a business big enough that other people were working for them on their boats.

Ships in biblical times were not very seaworthy. Most boats and ships were used for fishing on lakes (the "Sea" of Galilee is actually a large lake) or for taking goods up and down rivers like the Nile in Egypt. Even after the time of Christ, ships did not improve very much. The ship that took Paul to Rome couldn't handle a major storm. Paul's captain and all the crew were saved, but the ship went down despite the captain's knowledge of sailing.

Find out more about ships and sea captains. In the back of your Bible, look for passages with the words:

ship
shipwreck
fishing
sea

WORLDS
around us

The heavens tell of the glory of God. The skies display his marvelous craftsmanship.

PSALM 19:1

Jupiter floats in the airless sky of its giant moon Ganymede, where mountains wind across the ice surface.

Europa's cracked ice surface may hide a deep ocean. (Photo courtesy NASA/JPL)

Jupiter is the king. It can't sing like Elvis, but it's the biggest planet in our solar system. Jupiter is heavier than all the other planets and their moons put together! One thousand Earths could fit inside of it.

Jupiter has at least seventeen moons. Four of them are nearly as large as planets themselves. They are called the Galilean moons because they were discovered by Galileo through his newly invented telescope. Europa and Io (EYE-oh) are the size of Earth's moon. Ganymede and Callisto are about the size of the planet Mercury. Before 1979, astronomers thought Jupiter's moons were probably a lot like other small worlds, with cold, dead surfaces covered by craters. But then *Voyager* 1 and 2 flew by, taking snapshots of Jupiter, its faint rings, its bigger-than-earth storms, and—you guessed it—its moons. What they found blew them away.

Callisto and Ganymede do have craters, but Ganymede has vast mountains that look like piles of spaghetti lying across its frozen surface. Smaller Europa is even weirder. It has almost no craters and looks more like a jumbled hockey rink. Its ice surface is broken and twisted into beautiful patterns of lines and cracks. Many believe there is an ocean of water under the ice of Europa.

A volcano blasts nearly two hundred miles into space above Jupiter's volcanically active moon, Io. (Photo courtesy NASA/JPL)

But the real surprise is Io. Little Io is the most violent heavenly body we've ever checked out. Its orange and yellow volcanoes blast sulfur two hundred miles into its airless sky! Io's landscape is becoming so messed up by volcanoes that our maps of it will be all wrong in three hundred years! Space specialists thought Io would be a dead sphere, but the gravity of Jupiter and the other moons pushes and pulls Io so that its insides heat up "big time." The heat explodes out as "mega-volcanoes."

Scientists were surprised by how wonderful, strange, different, radical, ultra-mega-hyper-extreme Jupiter's moons turned out to be. The scientists' concept of these moons was too simple, too small.

Our view of God is also too small. Even John, who lived for three years with God's Son, Jesus, had too small a view of God. When John was an old man, he prayed for his friend, the carpenter, to come back. But he saw Jesus show up in glory and power instead. God is greater than our little minds can understand. Like the moons of Jupiter, he is more wonderful, strange, different, radical, and ultra-mega-hyper-extreme than our micro-brains can even imagine. Praise God!

Think about what God says to you

*When I saw him, I fell at his feet as dead.
But he laid his right hand on me and said,
"Don't be afraid! I am the First and the Last."*
REVELATION 1:17

So often, we think of God as too small or too far away or too mysterious to help us with our problems. But if we really get to know him, we can see a clearer picture of him in our minds. That picture develops as we talk to him in prayer and read about him in the Bible. God wants us to know the real him!

Let's talk to God!

MY JOURNAL (choose one)

God, it's hard for me to believe you are powerful enough to handle this:

_____

_____

_____

_____

This is something about you, God, that I would like to have a clearer picture of:

_____

_____

_____

_____

MY PRAYER

Lord God, you rule the universe, you know everything, you live forever, you can be everywhere at the same time, you can do everything, and you never change. Wow! Help me to understand just a little more about you today.

Night Sky

Choose a clear night and go outside with your mom or dad, taking a pair of binoculars. What is the biggest, brightest object you can see in the sky? If it's not the moon, it's one of the planets: Venus, Jupiter, Saturn, or Mars. These planets appear as the brightest "stars" in the sky.

Saturn, the golden giant world, has the most beautiful rings of any planet, but flying through them would be deadly. (Photo courtesy of R. Beebe, New Mexico State University; D. Gilmore, L. Bergeron, Space Telescope Science Institute; and NASA)

One of the most beautiful worlds around is the golden-ringed giant, Saturn. Four planets have rings (Jupiter, Saturn, Uranus, and Neptune), but Saturn's rings are by far the biggest and most beautiful. From the inside to the outside edges of the rings—just one side—you could lay sixty-seven countries the size of the United States end to end.

The rings are like a great disk of asteroids and boulders moving as fast as bullets. They aren't solid, but you can't fly through them. At the speed they are moving, a tiny particle of rock from the rings could go right through your spaceship—or through you! When *Voyager 2* flew by Saturn in 1981, it had to fly through the Cassini Division, a clear gap in the rings. Even there it was battered by tiny particles of dust and sand.

The magnificent rings stretch over the golden clouds of Saturn like a shimmering rainbow. The rings have mysterious "spokes" of dust that float around the planet like spokes on a wheel. The rocks in the rings may be mostly ice, for they are bright white in the sunlight. If you could somehow float inside them, you might be able to see a halo around the sun and many strange colors reflecting off the icy chunks. This is truly one of the most extraordinary places in God's creation. "It rocks."

The rings of Saturn seem very beautiful, but they are deadly. Many things in the world are like that—they appear too good to be true but really are not good at all. For example, in some philosophies and religions, people believe that if you wish for something, it will happen that way. "Make your own reality," they say. That sounds good. But wishing something to be one way doesn't make it so. It makes us act as if we're little gods who can control the world around us. That is not good. It is God who makes reality; as his creation, we must not try to be the Creator.

In today's society there are many beliefs and few rules. "Whatever" is the order of the day. However, God's laws can guide us safely through the asteroid fields of other beliefs. Only God has shown us the real truth in his Son, Jesus Christ.

Think about what God says to you

And the people of Berea were more open-minded than those in Thessalonica, and they listened eagerly to Paul's message. They searched the Scriptures day after day to check up on Paul and Silas, to see if they were really teaching the truth.
ACTS 17:11

Our world is filled with wonderful people who believe many things. While God calls us to love and respect each other, we don't have to believe everything that the people around us say. The truth about us, our world, and our God is in the Bible. As we try to figure out the world around us, it is good to compare our beliefs to what the Bible says. If we are in agreement—great. If the Bible is silent about the things we are trying to figure out, we can pray for God's wisdom to help us figure out as much as we can. If what the people around us believe is different from what God's Word says, watch out! The other beliefs are certainly wrong, because the Bible, which is a message from the Creator of the whole universe, is certainly right!

Let's talk to God!

MY JOURNAL (choose one)

Something I have heard from other people that is the opposite of what your Word teaches is:

_____

_____

_____

_____

Here is what I could say to help a friend who believes something that isn't true:

_____

_____

_____

_____

MY PRAYER

Thank you, God, for giving us the truth in the Bible. I believe that your Word tells the truth, no matter what anybody else thinks or says. Help me to be excited about reading it, learning about it, and sharing its Good News with my friends.

Iapetus, one of Saturn's strange moons, has one face as white as snow and another as dark as the asphalt on a parking lot. (*Voyager 2* photo, courtesy NASA/JPL)

In addition to having the most beautiful rings, Saturn also is the planet with the most moons—twenty-one at last count! As we discussed two days ago, the largest moons belong to Jupiter, with Ganymede and Callisto being about the size of the planet Mercury. Saturn's biggest moon is Titan, which is nearly as large as Ganymede. Titan has atmosphere (like most fancy restaurants!). But one of Saturn's smaller moons has a great mystery. It's Iapetus, a tiny ball a little less than half the size of our moon. But the mystery is in its face or, rather, two faces.

One side of Iapetus is as bright as dirty snow, while the other side is as dark as the asphalt on a parking lot. We have only fuzzy views of this moon now, but what we have seen is a real "bizarro" puzzler. Some people think the dark stuff is a coating that rained down on the icy surface of Iapetus. But where did it come from? Others look at the craters and see that some are filled with the dark stuff, like a bowl of brown cereal. Maybe, they think, this substance is coming from inside, like gooey volcanoes. If you look carefully at the dark edge of Iapetus, some darkness seems to be coming up from inside, staining its white surface.

Our sin is a lot like that dark side of Iapetus. (If a moon could be sinful, there might be cause for suspicion!) We run around with nice clothes and smiles on our faces, wearing a bright surface like one face of Iapetus. But the fact is, we all have done sinful things. We tell little white lies, or we don't do what we say we will. Deep inside us we hold on to hate for somebody, or we stay angry because it's easier than saying, "Sorry, I blew it." But sin is a funny thing. If we give it enough time, it always comes to the surface and stains that white covering of ours.

God wants us to come clean so he can help us clean up the mess we've made. Is there something you did that needs undoing? Do it! And always remember, you can't mess up anything that God can't clean up. He will help you to not do it again, and life will be excellent.

Think about what God says to you

You spread out our sins before you—
our secret sins—and you see them all.
PSALM 90:8

We like to think that if our sin doesn't hurt anybody and nobody knows about it, then it will not matter. We can ignore the sin, and it will go away, right? Wrong. God sees all of our sin, just as he sees all the good things we do. But even our most secret sins are obvious to God—as obvious as if they were spread out on a table. As long as we really are sorry for our sin and ask God to help us to not do it again, God forgives us. God is aware that we all are sinners, and he loves us anyway! Knowing this helps us to be honest with God.

Let's talk to God!

MY JOURNAL (choose one)

Here is one sin I have put off telling you about:

_____

_____

_____

I have asked you to forgive me for this, but I need you to help me not to do it anymore:

_____

_____

_____

_____

MY PRAYER

Thank you for being patient with me, Lord, when I put off asking you to forgive me for something bad I've said or done. Help me not to be two-faced with you. When I sin, I want to tell you right away instead of stalling around and acting as if everything is fine when it isn't.

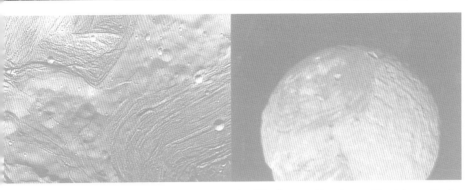

Some of the most bizarre places on Uranus's mixed-up moon Miranda can be seen here. This view of grooves and ridges is about 140 miles across. (*Voyager 2* photo, courtesy NASA/JPL)

Just 300 miles across, Uranus's moon Miranda is exceptionally bizarre. In its childhood, Miranda was probably mixed up by a massive asteroid that smacked it as it was forming. (Photo courtesy NASA/JPL)

Our planetary wanderings take us now into the dark outer solar system, where the sun is more like a superbright star. Out here lies the "jolly green giant," Uranus. Uranus doesn't spin around like the other planets. It is tipped over on its side so that it sort of rolls as it travels around the sun. And rolling around it are fifteen moons. One of these moons is crazy and mixed up. Totally.

Everybody thought Miranda would be a quiet little moon with lots of little craters and not much else. Miranda is small for a moon: You could drive all the way around it in about twenty-four hours. It should be a calm place.

A moon or planet starts out as a bunch of rock and lighter stuff— ice, if you are a moon in the outer solar system. The heavy material sinks to the bottom, and the light stuff forms a crust on top. Then it all cools down and stays that way. Not Miranda. No way. Miranda turns out to be all mixed up from the inside out.

Planetary scientists think that when Miranda had almost settled down, with its rocks in the middle and ice on the outside, it got smacked by an asteroid. It has the scars to show for it: rocks where the ice should be, ice deep down, wrinkles, and bumps. Poor, confused little moonlet.

People can also be mixed up. And they can be spiritually damaged, even when they look as if they have it together on the outside. A lot of things in life can confuse us, and sometimes things hurt us, too. God has a special love for people who are hurting and unhappy. Fortunately, we are not frozen into this state the way Miranda is. God is a giver of second chances. When we call his number, he warms us up and resurfaces us. Instead of leaving us frozen in our old ways, he makes us new.

Think about what God says to you

You keep track of all my sorrows.
You have collected all my tears in your bottle.
You have recorded each one in your book.
PSALM 56:8

This is a great verse to read when you are hurting, or to share with a friend who is unhappy. It tells us that God is not ignoring us when we are sad or in pain. He counts every tear we shed and reaches out to comfort us.

Let's talk to God!

MY JOURNAL (choose one)
Here is something that is making me feel mixed up and sad, and I need your help so I don't keep feeling this way:

_____

_____

_____

This is someone I know who is all mixed up like Miranda, and I would like you to help me think of a way to help this person get to know you:

_____

_____

_____

_____

MY PRAYER

Dear God, you are never far away from us. You are close enough to count every tear we shed. Thank you for comforting me. Now I want to reach out to someone I know who is sad, and tell that person about your love and care.

Mixed-Up Miranda

Take a two-cup, clear plastic or glass container and put in one-fourth cup dry beans (big rocks), one-fourth cup brown rice or pearl barley (small rocks), and two tablespoons white flour (ice). Pour in one cup water. If the container has a lid, put the lid on and shake it. If not, stir well with a spoon. Then take "Miranda" outside and let it sit for twenty minutes. Look carefully at the layers that have formed. Now find a heavy rubber ball (asteroid) and drop it into Miranda's surface from a height of about four feet. *Splat!* What happens to Miranda's nice layers?

Nobody has ever seen Pluto up close, but it may look a lot like this moon of Neptune, called Triton. Pluto is the same size and hangs out in the same part of the solar system a lot of the time. (*Voyager 2* photo, courtesy NASA/JPL)

The most distant planet yet found in our solar system is Pluto. No, Pluto was not named after Mickey's dog. It bears the name of the mythological god of the underworld, a world of darkness and loneliness. It's a perfect name. Pluto's orbit carries it so far from the sun that most of the air around it turns into solid ice that freezes to the surface. The nitrogen that is part of the air we breathe on Earth is pink ice on Pluto. Pluto, which is forty times as far from the sun as we are, takes 248 years to go around the sun one time! In this lonely neighborhood, the day is only a dim twilight, and summertime heat waves clock in at about 350 degrees below zero Fahrenheit!

We have never seen its surface clearly, but we have seen a close cousin: Neptune's moon Triton. Triton is as far from the sun as Pluto is for much of the planet's orbit, although Pluto's egg-shaped path takes it out much farther. In fact, sometimes Pluto is actually closer than Neptune and Triton but never for long. Triton is a strange world of icy volcanoes, frozen atmosphere, and seasons that last forty years. We will probably discover someday that Pluto is similar, but with surprises of its own. No doubt. And there may be a few smaller planets even farther out.

Pluto is so far from the heat, light, and energy of the sun that we can assume it is a cold, dead place. We on Earth take for granted warm, sunny days filled with living things all around us. However, as we make our way through the solar system, looking at places that are farther and farther away from the sun, we see that things begin to slow down. Water is frozen most of the time, and places become dead, like Pluto.

In our day-to-day personal trip through life, God is like the sun to our soul. He is the source of energy deep within us. If we move away from God, our life becomes cold and dark, and it's much harder to see clearly up ahead. Are you feeling a little lost? A little cold or frustrated? Maybe you need to get closer to the light and warmth of God. He is waiting for you!

Think about what God says to you

Draw close to God, and God will draw close to you.
When you bow down before the Lord and admit your
dependence on him, he will lift you up and give you honor.
JAMES 4:8, 10

Like Pluto, we can wander into an orbit that takes us far away from God. But no matter how frustrated and lost we feel, God wants us to come back and be close to him so that we can feel his warmth and powerful love. All of this will be real to us every day if we talk to him, read his Word, and live to please him.

Let's talk to God!

MY JOURNAL (choose one)
This is something that tempts me to do things that do not please God and that make me feel confused or lost:

_____

_____

_____

This is something I need to do to get closer to God:

_____

_____

_____

_____

MY PRAYER

Lord, help me to not hang with people who take me away from you. Help me to enjoy the things in life that you want me to spend time on. Help me to stay near you and feel your power when I am confused, lonely, or hurt.

Space Riddles

Q: What is the favorite sandwich of a space scientist?
A: Pastronomy on rye.

Q: If athletes get athlete's foot, what do astronauts get?
A: Missile toe.

Q: What is at the center of gravity?
A: The letter V.

Q: How did the astronomer describe the exploding star?
A: Sphere today, gone tomorrow.

Q: Where would you find a list of dead planets?
A: In the orbit-uary column.

MARS

the radical desert world

Who created a channel for the torrents of rain? Who laid out the path for the lightning? Who makes the rain fall on barren land, in a desert where no one lives?

JOB 38: 25-26

An asteroid slams into Mars, sending steam and dust into the salmon-colored sky. Water rushes out onto the surface, but it will be gone soon in the thin, cold air.

This Martian valley has a dried-up riverbed running through the middle of it. (Mars Global Surveyor image, courtesy NASA/JPL)

Mars is over 50 million miles from home. It's half as big as our own world, and it's tough to see through even the most gargantuan telescopes. One hundred years ago an astronomer guy named Percival Lowell thought people lived on Mars. In fact, tons of people thought so back then. The blurry views through Lowell's scope gave him the idea that the Red Planet must be inhabited by a croaking race of Martians who dug canals to bring water from the snowy polar caps to the deserts. It's no wonder that so many were fooled. Each spring the polar caps melt and shrink, and a mysterious dark wave moves across Mars, looking like veggies are growing from melting water. But when spacecraft finally scoped out the Red Planet, we found that Mars is a desert world with dark sands that blow with the seasons, causing the dark wave Lowell saw.

Lowell's mistaken beliefs caused him to see the Mars that he wanted to see. But things aren't always what they seem.

How many times do we see God the way we want to see him, through our own "spiritual telescope"? And how small the god of our minds can be! Yet Jesus gives us a clear view of God. If we take a little time to "sit at his feet" each day by reading the Bible and praying, the eternal, infinite, almighty, *real* God will speak to us. The true God of the universe will replace the tiny god that sometimes creeps into our minds. We'll discover that this eternal, infinite God really cares about us. He actually wants to let us in on his thoughts and plans!

Think about what God says to you

> *We who have the Spirit understand these things,*
> *but others can't understand us at all.*
>
> 1 CORINTHIANS 2:15

So often we think of God as too small or too far away to help us
with our problems. God seems mysterious. The book of Job asks,
"Can you solve the mysteries of God? Can you discover everything
there is to know about the Almighty?" (Job 11:7) But as we let the
Holy Spirit help us get to know God the Father, we will have a
clearer picture of God in our minds. God wants us to know the real
him!

Let's talk to God!

MY JOURNAL (choose one)

God, here is something that I don't understand about you:

_____

_____

_____

_____

Lord, I need your help to figure out this part of my personal life:

_____

_____

_____

_____

Here is a person or circumstance that I don't understand:

_____

_____

_____

_____

MY PRAYER

God, help me to remember that you are greater, bigger, and more power-ful than anything I've ever seen. Thank you for loving me and caring about the problems in my life today.

Percival Lowell's Telescope

Find an empty paper-towel or toilet-paper tube. Crinkle up three or four baggies, then smooth them out and put them over the end of the tube, fastening them with a rubber band. Now look at various things through your "telescope." Imagine you are trying to describe something you have never seen before, just like Percival Lowell did. Notice how the things you look at appear different from the way they really are. The Bible tells us that until we go to live with God in heaven, he is like this to us. We try to imagine him, but we can't really see him clearly. Paul the apostle said, "Now we see things imperfectly as in a poor mirror, but then we will see everything with perfect clarity" (1 Corinthians 13:12).

DAY 2: OCEANS INTO DESERTS

The Mars Pathfinder's rover, Sojourner, checks out a Martian rock. (Photo courtesy NASA/JPL)

Mars is a planet of awesome sand dunes, "honkin' " giant volcanoes, and bizarre craters. If you like surfing, you'd better go somewhere else. It never rains, and the skimpy snow that falls is mostly frozen carbon dioxide (just like the "dry ice" at the ice cream store). Nobody's been for a swim on Mars in a long time, but it wasn't always that way. Dry river valleys wander through ancient craters and rugged mountains. Some people think these places were carved by floods. Others say that oceans or glaciers may have covered the smooth northern plains for a while. Whatever happened, Mars must have been much wetter when it was a "kid" than it is today. But something made the water dry up, and most of the air drifted off into space.

If you like to breathe, Mars isn't your kind of place either. The air is one hundred times thinner than on Earth. It's truly a frozen desert, more dreary than the Judean desert Christ knew so well.

At the beginning of his ministry, Jesus hiked into the desert for forty days and nights. Out there he went head-to-head with the Devil, and he won! Oh yes, he won BIG!

The desert has often been a special place for God's people.

Sometimes God takes us through a sort of "spiritual desert." Suddenly we find ourselves in a place where God seems distant and silent, and where life is no fun anymore. But it is in these dry times, these spiritual deserts, that God does his most incredible stuff. God's greatest silence in history was during the four hundred years between the Old and New Testament. In this silence, the Lord was preparing for the most radical part of his plan for people: the Messiah!

Are you going through a spiritual desert? In the silence, God is still working. He may be getting you ready for a special and wonderful new chapter in your life. The richest lessons that God wants us to learn—patience, kindness, humility—can be found only in the places we would rather not go. Be patient with God. He doesn't forget his kids!

Water, water everywhere?

On July 4, 1997, the Pathfinder *lander and its little rover,* Sojourner, *slammed into Mars inside a bunch of airbags. After checking out the place for a day or so, the lander let* Sojourner *loose to scope out the place. Pathfinder's new home was in a place called Ares Valley. And even though there's not a drop to drink now, the place had an extreme flood a long time ago. Mars gurus think Ares Valley was carved out by more water than is found in all of the Great Lakes put together. That would make a cube of water about 186 miles wide, high, and deep! Mars is bone dry now. Where did all the water go? It's just another Mars mystery!*

Think about what God says to you

For forty years I [God] led you through the wilderness, yet your clothes and sandals did not wear out. . . . He gave you food so you would know that he is the Lord your God.

DEUTERONOMY 29:5-6

Sometimes it seems as if God is nowhere to be seen in our personal little world. We wander around as if we're alone in the desert. God kept the Hebrews safe while he led them through the wilderness. Even when they were lonely and confused and lost, God took care of them. God is taking care of us, even when we can't tell he's there.

Let's talk to God!

MY JOURNAL (choose one)

God, here is something that I am impatient about. Help me to have peace about this:

_____

_____

_____

_____

Lord, thank you for helping me see now that you were with me even when:

_____

_____

_____

_____

MY PRAYER

God, sometimes it seems as if you aren't near me. Let me feel your closeness to me. Bring me out of my own deserts as a stronger person and a stronger follower of your Son.

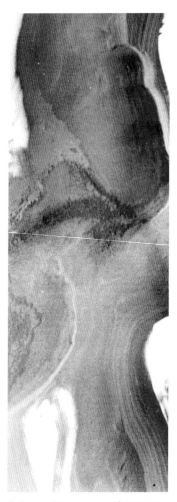

God has used Martian dust and frozen carbon dioxide to sculpt one of the most awesome places on any world. (Viking photo, courtesy NASA/JPL)

Beyond the wintry deserts of Mars, across a vast ring of black sand dunes, lies the brilliant white north polar ice cap. From space, the ice cap looks as if somebody sneaked in and pinstriped the snow. Graceful brown lines swirl across the shimmering ice. But this beautiful place has nasty weather. Temperatures drop to less than minus two hundred degrees Fahrenheit each night. And if the air were any thicker, the winds would blow you away! Searing gusts cut across the frozen fields at nearly supersonic speeds. Relentless snows of dry ice (frozen carbon dioxide) seal the orange Martian dust in underground layers.

But on Mars the Lord has sculpted cold harshness into a place of complete beauty. The winds expose the layers of dust and ice, carving out a thousand miles of layered cliffs like nothing on any other world.

Each of us has a cold place in our lives—a crabby neighbor we don't get along with, a tough teacher, or a diffi-cult relationship with a parent or two. Sometimes we let these cold places harden, just like the dry ice of Mars. But the God of the universe can sculpt even the coldest places inside us. He's a "righteous" artist! In time he can make something really beautiful out of the ice and dust.

Think about what God says to you

> *Lord, be merciful to us, for we have waited for you.*
> *Be our strength each day and our salvation in times of trouble.*
> ISAIAH 33:2

Even on really bad days, God can be our strength if we learn to lean on him.

Let's talk to God!

MY JOURNAL (choose one)

God, this is a "cold place" in my life, a thing that is bothering me; I know you can make it better:

_____

_____

_____

_____

_____ is a person who is "cold" to me, a person whom I don't get along with right now. Reach down from heaven and change our relationship so that we can be friends. Change my attitude, and change this person's heart too.

MY PRAYER

Lord, take this cold place in my life and blow your warm Spirit across it. Make it a beautiful thing, and give me the chance to help others who feel cold and alone.

Mars Polar Cap

The beautiful stripes of the Martian polar caps are made by layers of dust and ice. Get two or three different colors of clay. Flatten them out into thin layers, then put them on top of each other so that you have six or eight layers of clay. Take a butter knife and carefully slice off the edge at an angle. You will see layers much as we can see in the polar cliffs of Mars. Instead of the butter knife, Mars has winds that cut into the layers and expose the beautiful stripes. Compare the beautiful cross section of your clay cliff to the boring top of it. Often there is beauty inside of people who seem blah and boring too.

DAY 4: OLYMPUS MONS

The largest mountain in the solar system is the volcano Olympus Mons, which towers above the Martian plains two and one-half times as tall as Mount Everest. (Viking 2 photo, courtesy NASA/JPL)

By far the hugest mountain on Mars, far larger than anything on Earth or any other place in our solar system, is the great volcano, Olympus Mons. It towers two and a half times higher than Mount Everest, and its base would completely cover the state of Arizona. Olympus Mons is the kind of place that astronauts dream of climbing, just as Sir Edmund Hillary and Tensing Norgay did, so that they were the first to climb the slopes of Mount Everest.

Mountains have been important not only to humans but to God's plan as well. God appeared to Moses and Elijah on mountaintops, Noah's ark came to rest on one, and Jesus took three of his disciples to the top of a mountain.

When people have a really awesome thing happen to them, or when they have the "mack daddy of cool times," they call it a "mountaintop experience." God brings us through many mountaintop experiences to make us strong and brave.

Think about what God says to you

Six days later Jesus took Peter, James, and John to the top of a mountain. No one else was there. As the men watched, Jesus' appearance changed, and his clothing became dazzling white.... "Teacher, this is wonderful!" Peter exclaimed.

MARK 9:2-3, 5

Jesus provided three of his disciples a mountaintop experience when they witnessed the Transfiguration. Peter wanted to stay on the mountain, saying, "This is wonderful!" But Jesus hadn't brought his three closest friends to the top of the mountain to take them out of the world. He wanted them to go on back down that slope with the strength they gained from their experience.

God teaches us many things through our experiences. But he expects us to take the gifts he gives us in the "jammin'" times and head back to our regular lives as better people. His plan is for us to share the things we learn with our "buds."

Let's talk to God!

MY JOURNAL (choose one)

God, this experience helped me see how powerful you are:

_____

_____

_____

_____

God, this experience helped me understand how much you care
about me:

_____

_____

_____

_____

MY PRAYER

Lord, I thank you for the times you have shown me your great wonders.
Help me to never forget the super stuff you have told me in your Word.
When I don't feel like skipping with joy, help me to remember the moun-
taintops and think about how good you are.

Surfing and Visiting

Cyber-surf Mars or visit a planetarium to get the latest news from
Mars. You can get great news and images from:

- the Web site for Mars Global Surveyor at http://www.msss.com/
- the Web site for all the photos and information from the
  Pathfinder mission at http://mars.nlanr.net/mpf-splash.html
- the Web site for NASA's planet photos at
  http://photojournal.jpl.nasa.gov

Mars's largest moon, Phobos (shown here), and Deimos are both so small that they look more like giant rocks than little moons. (Mars Global Surveyor photo, courtesy NASA/JPL)

Genesis 1:16 tells us that "God made two great lights, the sun and the moon, to shine down upon the earth." But in the case of Mars, God created three "great lights"—the sun for the day and two moons for the night. The moons are called Phobos and Deimos. Lucky Mars!

Less than twenty-five miles across, neither little moon is round. They both look like beat-up gray potatoes. Deimos circles Mars far away, while Phobos spins around the planet much closer and in the opposite direction! From the ground Phobos appears to rise in the west as Deimos sets there. Phobos dashes overhead, changing from a crescent to a full moon, then disappears behind the eastern horizon, only to come up again three and a half hours later. Deimos is more laid back, making its east-to-west trip around Mars in just over a day. The tweaked paths that these moons take and the strange way they look tell us that they're probably asteroids that wandered too near Mars and were snatched by its gravity. They are cosmic drifters, caught by Mars and now settled down to stay and "chill" for a while.

Gravity also affects people living on Earth. However, it is not the only influence in our lives. Without God we are blown this way and that by the stuff in life. Each one of us worries: Am I popular? What do my friends think of me? How good do I look? But when we let God speak to us, we're free from the worries that life throws our way. God starts us on a new path. Some of us race into it like Phobos. Others are drawn in at a more easy pace, like Deimos. But when we finally arrive at the place where we allow Christ to come into our lives, our direction is changed forever. No matter where we come from or how beat-up we may look, he takes us to his side, changes our path, and sends us off toward a better place.

Heavy, Dude!

The smaller a planet or moon is, the less gravity it has. Mars has about one-third the gravity Earth has, so if you weigh one hundred pounds on Earth, you would weigh about thirty-three on Mars.

Mars's big potato moon, Phobos, is so small that it has almost no gravity. You would weigh three thousand times less on Phobos than you do on Earth! You could jump three thousand times higher and carry three thousand times more. Things bounce around and barely hang on to the ground of this little moon. If you could stand in one place there and toss a baseball really hard, you would see it bounce and bounce until it disappeared over the faraway hills. If you threw it straight enough, you could wait a few hours, turn around, and watch it come back to you after it went all the way around the moon on which you were standing! (Don't expect this to work on Earth.)

Think about what God says to you

> Do not be afraid, for I have ransomed you.
> I have called you by name; you are mine.
>
> ISAIAH 43:1

When we realize our need to follow Christ and get on the path God wants us to take, we are his. He knows us by name and loves us. We belong to him, and he sets us free to be his children.

Let's talk to God!

MY JOURNAL

God, please show me the direction you want me to go in my life. I know you speak to me through prayer, the wisdom of other Christ-followers, and life's circumstances. Help me to hear your voice in these things, and show me what I should do about this:

_____

_____

_____

_____

MY PRAYER

Lord, thank you for changing the path of my life. Help me to see the places you want me to go, and show me how to help others find your way.

End-of-the-Week Word Search
Find the following words and phrases:

CRATERS
DEIMOS
GOD IS AWESOME
ICE CAP
MARS IS COOL
OLYMPUS
PERCIVAL LOWELL

PHOBOS
PLANET
RED PLANET
SCOPE
VIEW
VOLCANO

```
P  G  O  D  I  S  A  W  E  S  O  M  E  S
C  B  H  S  D  R  R  V  S  B  U  K  Q  C
S  F  O  L  A  N  G  W  I  T  E  A  R  O
O  N  A  C  L  O  V  Q  T  E  X  P  U  P
R  L  C  D  C  H  K  I  R  E  W  M  C  E
E  D  R  A  S  E  A  C  P  U  M  P  R  G
D  S  L  O  O  F  T  E  T  D  R  E  A  O
P  G  R  T  B  L  S  C  W  E  C  S  T  R
L  L  E  W  O  L  L  A  V  I  C  R  E  P
A  C  W  M  H  B  A  P  U  M  V  O  R  F
N  B  S  B  P  N  E  N  Y  O  A  E  S  G
E  M  R  O  L  Y  M  P  U  S  C  E  V  U
T  E  N  A  L  P  E  D  D  P  Y  F  R  O
I  C  M  A  R  S  I  S  C  O  O  L  M  H
```

What does each word have to do with our devotionals this week?
How does each word, name, or phrase remind you of yourself? of God?
Always remember: Mars is cool, and God is awesome!

it is a SMALL WORLD after all

[The Kingdom of God] is like a tiny mustard seed. Though this is one of the smallest of seeds, it grows to become one of the largest of plants, with long branches where birds can come and find shelter.

MARK 4: 31-32

Nearly microscopic plants form a surreal landscape. Mosses and fungus live together to form lichen.

DAY 1: POND SCUM

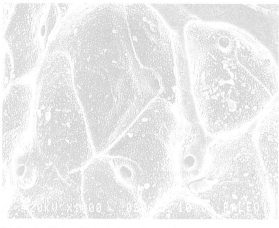

This Scanning Electron Microscope image shows a tiny armored creature one thousand times its normal size.

There are puddles and ponds all over the place, and they can get pretty gross—green crust on the edges and black gunk on the bottom. Mmmmm . . . is it soup yet?

There's more to these smelly mini-lakes than you can see, however. Within these ponds is a miniature universe of bizarre creatures. Believe it—there are tons of single-celled plants and animals that you can see only through a microscope. Even though they are tiny, they're extraordinary.

Take the hydra. It's got a long, blobby body that looks like a tube, and a bunch of arms that wave around and grab micro-meals. It's named after the Hydra from Greek legend, a many-headed monster that Hercules killed. (And you thought two heads were better than one.)

Then there's the paramecium. It looks like a clear balloon with hair all over it. A paramecium swims with its hair. (Ever tried that? It's not easy.)

All these strange beasties appear in water that doesn't move and is stagnant. If the pond doesn't get fresh water, scum grows!

Sin is like scum. People all have sin in their lives—things they do even though they know they shouldn't, and things they don't do even though they know they should.

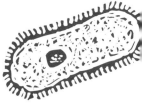

Think about what God says to you

> *If we confess our sins to him, he is faithful and just to forgive us and to cleanse us from every wrong.*
> *I JOHN 1:9*

It's so important to clean up our act by talking to God about our sins before they multiply and turn into very bad, scummy habits. God rejoices when we ask him to help clean the sin out of our lives to make room for him.

Let's talk to God!

MY JOURNAL (choose one)

This is something that's turning into a bad habit in my life, Lord, and I need you to help me with it:

_____

_____

_____

_____

I'm happy because you helped me get rid of this bad habit:

_____

_____

_____

_____

MY PRAYER

Show me how to be honest with you, Lord, about things I have done that make you sad, or things I need to be doing but don't seem to get around to. I know you will help me "clean house" and keep my heart clean if I ask you to.

Scanning Electron Microscope photo of a diatom. (Photo courtesy Scott Elias)

Many of the creatures in pond scum are so tiny that they have only one cell for their whole "bod!" As we saw yesterday, single-celled animals come in all sorts of weird and wacky forms. There are lots of single-celled plants, too. Some of the most beautiful are called diatoms.

Diatoms live with lots of other tiny ocean creatures in floating undersea clouds called plankton. Plankton is totally important to everybody on Earth. That's because it is food for the little creatures that are eaten by the bigger creatures, which are then eaten by the really big guys. We are munching away in there somewhere too. The single-celled plants in the world's oceans produce a *huge* amount of oxygen—the gas our bodies like to breathe. All these teensy plants are doing us a humungous favor, and we can't even see them to say, "Thanks, dude!"

Of all the living creatures found in plankton, the diatoms are the snazziest. Each one is like an etched jewel or crystal. Some look like bicycle reflectors, and others are more like needles or hard Christmas candy with ribs and facets. And they are beyond tiny. If you laid one thousand of them end to end, they would barely cover an inch of space! Even though from far away they look like, well, pond scum, these tiny treasures glow and sparkle in the light of a microscope.

Diatoms actually grow crystal boxes around their bodies. When a diatom outgrows its box, it splits, making itself into two. Except for their size, these new creatures look identical to their parent. In a month one diatom can multiply into a billion new ones, each a twin! (Or is that a "billionuplet"?) Imagine, a billion glowing, identical jewels floating in a lake or sea. That's diatoms for you.

Christ came into the world to make followers—people who would be like him. When he first started doing his thing, Christ picked twelve disciples. They stayed with him for three years. They ate with him and slept by him and traveled with him so that they began to feel the way Jesus did about life. They learned to be loving, patient, and kind—all the things Jesus was. Then they started making disciples. They multiplied! Like a cosmic diatom, Christ came to make us more like himself so that we could live our lives to the extreme. And when we have his joy and power in ourselves, he wants us to share it the way he did, the way his first twelve did, so that others can become Christ-followers too. So now, guess what? It's your turn to multiply and make disciples!

Think about what God says to you

Take this message of repentance to all the nations . . . :
"There is forgiveness of sins for all who turn to me."
LUKE 24:47

Talking to your friends about Jesus may feel a little weird at first if you've never done it before, but soon it will get easier. Just tell them what he's like and what he's doing in your life. Tell them that as the Son of God, he helped to create the world. Tell them that Jesus can forgive our sins and make us part of God's own family. You can tell about God the Father and God the Son just like you'd tell about your mom, your dad, or your brothers and sisters. After all, God's family is your family, too!

Let's talk to God!

MY JOURNAL (choose one)

Lord, this is how I feel when I think about talking to my friends about you:

_____

_____

_____

_____

This is a way you have helped me, Jesus, and I want to tell my friends about it:

_____

_____

_____

_____

MY PRAYER

Lord, I want to talk about you more and more each day as you become a bigger and more important part of my life. Help me to "just do it!"

DAY 3: DeoxyriboNucleic Acid

Have you ever tried to make two things exactly the same? Say, two clay giraffes, or two drawings of a face? It's not easy. The best way is to push clay into a mold or to trace around a picture you want to copy, so that each new item looks like the last.

Have you ever wondered why babies always come out looking like the parents? why baby gorillas look like gorillas, baby elephants look like elephants, and so on? It's because creatures are made up of cells, each of which has a blueprint or instruction book on how to build another creature like the last.

People also are made up of cells. Each person is an individual, made special and unlike anyone else. Still, you can tell that people are people just by looking at them: two eyes, two legs, one head—you get the drift. It's all because of the blueprint that God has put into the cells of each one of us.

This blueprint is called DNA. It stands for DeoxyriboNucleic Acid. (And there will be a quiz—just kidding!) Now you know why most people call it DNA instead of Deoxy . . . well, you know. DNA is found in each and every cell that makes up your body, and your DNA is different from everyone else's. DNA looks like two chains spiraling around each other in a microscopic dance. Inside of these coils is a map of you! When your cells reproduce to make more skin or bone or whatever they need to make, each cell makes an exact copy of the DNA. Sometimes disease is caused by DNA that breaks or doesn't copy itself right.

But as long as the DNA chain reproduces itself correctly, your body keeps humming along.

God wants us to look at Christ and copy him in our lives. He doesn't want us to try to copy the cool kids in class or the "Generation X" actors we see in videos. No way. We need to keep our eyes on God's Son.

Think about what God says to you

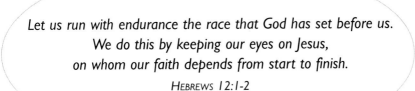

Let us run with endurance the race that God has set before us.
We do this by keeping our eyes on Jesus,
on whom our faith depends from start to finish.
HEBREWS 12:1-2

Don't get sidetracked by all the examples the world gives you to copy. They're all bogus. Jesus is the one to keep your eye on!

Let's talk to God!

MY JOURNAL (choose one)

This is somebody I am tempted to try to copy:

_____

_____

_____

_____

I'm tempted to copy this person because:

_____

_____

_____

_____

I need to copy Jesus by asking myself what he would do in this situation:

_____

_____

_____

_____

MY PRAYER

Father in heaven, I want to praise you and thank you for giving me Jesus as the example to copy in my life. As long as I keep my eyes on him, I won't stumble and I won't get lost.

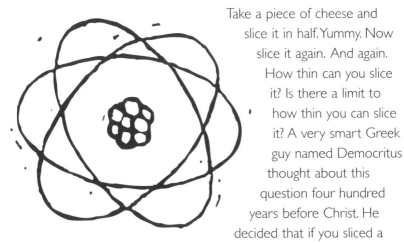

Take a piece of cheese and slice it in half. Yummy. Now slice it again. And again. How thin can you slice it? Is there a limit to how thin you can slice it? A very smart Greek guy named Democritus thought about this question four hundred years before Christ. He decided that if you sliced a piece of silver enough times, you'd finally get a tiny particle of silver that couldn't be cut anymore. This he called an atom. Democritus said, "The only existing things are atoms and empty space; all else is mere opinion." Not bad for a guy without a microscope!

Remember those atoms we checked out on Day 2 of Week 1? Look around you: everything you see—from water to clouds to your wooden kitchen table to the silverware on it to the burning sun outside—is made of a few simple kinds of building blocks called atoms. Each atom has a core, or nucleus. A hot dog is made of two important parts: the dog and the bun. A nucleus is made of two kinds of particles: protons and neutrons (although hot dogs are far easier to taste). If we could make an atom really big, say, the size of a football stadium, the protons and neutrons would be the size of golf balls huddled together, floating above the center of the fifty-yard line. Orbiting around them in a cloud the size of the outer walls of the stadium would be electrons. Electrons are very light compared to the heavy protons and neutrons of the nucleus, but nobody seems to mind this and it works well, so we won't let it bother us.

Protons, neutrons, and electrons are packets of energy. Try putting a solid cup on a solid table. What's really happening is that you are putting energy fields shaped like a cup on top of energy fields shaped like a table. Nothing you see is as solid as it looks. In fact, nothing on earth is solid. And if that makes you feel like you might just fall through the floor, no one would blame you!

Sometimes God doesn't seem solid, even though we know he's around here somewhere. But God is far more solid than that table or cup or anything we can see. The Bible tells us God is our rock. This world is not solid, and it will not last forever. But God will. If you want to feel something really solid, lean on him.

Think about what God says to you

> *The Lord is my rock, my fortress, and my savior;*
> *my God is my rock, in whom I find protection.*
> 2 SAMUEL 22:2-3

Rocks seem pretty solid. Along a rocky shoreline we can hold onto a rock for safety if the tide comes in and the water tries to sweep us away. But even rocks eventually crumble and disappear. Only God will never change and never leave.

Let's talk to God!

MY JOURNAL (choose one)

No one but you, God, could create the atoms that make up the universe and all the stuff in it. Thank you for putting atoms together to make these things:

_____

_____

Dear God, I need to lean on you, my solid rock, to help me with this:

_____

_____

_____

_____

MY PRAYER

Thank you for being my rock! You made everything, creating it all out of tiny building blocks called atoms. You made light where there was only darkness; water, earth, and air where there was nothing. I know I can count on you to protect me when everything else seems shaky.

Read about a Scientist Who Believes: Christian Physicist Randall Ingermansson

Randy Ingermansson is a physicist—a scientist who studies the nature of matter and energy. He says, "When we look at smaller and smaller things, we see how much trouble God took to make the universe an interesting place. He made a whole zoo of tiny little particles—all whizzing around in fuzzy little orbits, daring us to try to look at them. He made quarks and gluons tie themselves into three-dimensional knots to form neutrons and protons. And he made the smallest things we know about—superstrings—to be responsible for gravity, which holds the universe together! The tiny world inside a single atom is wonderfully complex. God must have had fun putting it all together into a weird, wild, wacky puzzle that we might solve some-day—maybe."

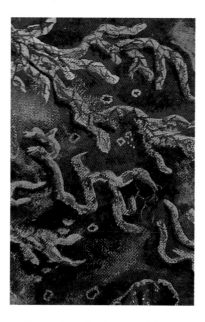

When atoms combine with each other, they make molecules. Molecules are a lot like the words on this page, with atoms being the letters that make up each word. Change one atom and you have a completely different molecule—sort of like changing one little letter in a word. For example, what's the difference between *desert* and *dessert?* (Answers: One "s" and a whole lot of sand. Riding a camel versus eating ice cream!) That one letter makes all the difference.

Even though they are bigger than single atoms, molecules are still tiny. Every molecule of water contains just three atoms: two hydrogen atoms stuck to one oxygen atom. But in one pint of water there is an unbelievable number of molecules. Picture the fact that there are eight pints in a gallon—take a look at the milk jug in your refrigerator. Now pretend you can take all the water molecules from just one pint and spread them out end to end. Those tiny molecules would circle our world 20 million times!

If several of the same kind of atoms combine, the stuff they make is called an element. The oxygen molecules we breathe are made of two oxygen atoms each: nitrogen is made of two nitrogen atoms; hydrogen has two hydrogen atoms. Get the picture? But when something is made of two or more different kinds of atoms, it is called a compound. As we just saw, when two atoms of hydrogen stick to one oxygen atom, you get a water molecule (which the fish are pretty happy about). Combine poisonous chlorine and poisonous sodium and you get salt (chlorine and sodium can kill you, but salt keeps you alive). Sugar has twelve carbon atoms, twenty-two hydrogen atoms, and eleven oxygen atoms. Sweet! Compounds can be broken down into their various atoms, but they just aren't the same anymore. If you break sugar down, the hydrogen and oxygen get together to become water, and then you have leftover carbon, but it's not something you would want to sprinkle on your cereal.

People are the same way spiritually. Like sugar without carbon, we are not complete without God. Our lives are empty without him. Some people try to fill that emptiness with money or computer games or fast cars or drugs, but that doesn't work for long. Hydrogen and oxygen atoms cannot combine with nitrogen atoms to make sugar. Only carbon will do. And only God, through Christ, will fill the hole in our souls. God makes us complete. He wants us to live full, happy lives. With God, we are like a complete molecule, stable and strong.

Think about what God says to you

And you are complete through your union with Christ.
Colossians 2:10

God promises us in his Word (Matthew 5:6) that if we hunger and thirst after what is right and good, he will fill us up and make us complete. But we've got to want to. Do you?

Let's talk to God!

MY JOURNAL (choose one)

God, this is a part of my life that feels kind of empty right now, and I'm asking you to fill it:

_____

_____

_____

_____

I see my unbelieving friends trying to fill up their emptiness in these ways:

_____

_____

_____

_____

MY PRAYER

Lord, help me remember that if I'm far from you, you're not the one who moved! Help me stay "bonded" to you just like the atoms that form molecules. When I am complete in you, together we can make something good.

The Molecule Splitter

You will need an adult with you to do this experiment. Get an old pie tin, a small glass jar with a wide mouth, and a tablespoon of sugar. Now get ready to split some molecules!

Put the pie tin on a burner on your stove, and put the tablespoon of sugar in a little pile in the center. Set the glass jar over the sugar and turn the burner on low heat. In about five minutes you'll notice something: steam is forming in the jar. When it starts making drops of liquid, take a pot holder and *carefully* set the jar on the stovetop, right side up. Wait a few minutes for the jar to cool, then stick your finger in and taste some of the liquid. It's water—not sweet at all.

A sugar molecule is a compound made up of three kinds of atoms: hydrogen, oxygen, and carbon. Heating the sugar caused the oxygen and hydrogen to combine together to make water.

Keep heating the sugar on the stove for a while until all the water is gone and it turns black. Use your pot holder again to take the pie tin off the burner. Let the pie tin cool a few minutes. Now taste the black stuff. Does it taste sweet? No, it tastes just like what it is—pure carbon!

Sharing Knowledge

Share with one of your friends what you've learned this week about all the tiny things God has made.

BUTTERFLIES

He flew, soaring on the wings of the wind.

2 SAMUEL 22:11

The strange life and times of the butterfly, from egg (lower left) to caterpillar to chrysalis to full-grown flier. This painting shows many different kinds of butterflies.

A butterfly shares a bouquet with a bee. (Photo courtesy Bill Gerrish)

As winter turns to spring, the brown valleys explode with green grass and wildflowers. The breeze brings a flurry of colors, fluttering in the sunlight, peppering the scene with tones even brighter than the flowers. Here come the butterflies!

Butterflies are outrageous and wonderful creatures. They smell with their antennae. They taste things with their feet. (Care for a walk through a chocolate sundae?)

Some of them can beat their wings forty times each second! And these winged beauties are the only bugs that have scales. These bugs belong to a type of insects called *Lepidoptera,* which is science-speak for "scaled wing." Butterflies have millions of tiny scales on their wings and body. The scales overlap like shingles on a roof, and these scales bring shimmering color to their wings. Butterflies wear every color of the rainbow. There are black and yellow swallowtails, glowing blue nymphalids, orange monarchs, blood red *Cymothoes,* and bright green *Malachites.*

But beneath the colorful scales, the wings of the butterfly are crystal clear. In fact, without these scales, all the world's seventeen thousand kinds of butterflies would look pretty much the same!

Why did God layer butterfly wings in such fabulous colors? Well, to bring himself glory—to put a little bit of his color and magnificence into these insects. And when we see the butterflies, we think of him!

We can bring glory to God too. How? By worshiping and praising him, and by becoming more like his wonderful Son, Jesus, in every-thing we say and do.

Think about what God says to you

> We can be mirrors that brightly reflect the glory of the Lord. And as the Spirit of the Lord works within us, we become more and more like him and reflect his glory even more.
>
> 2 CORINTHIANS 3:18

When the Holy Spirit helps us to be more like Jesus, it's as if we're getting new colors for our wings. Then a little more of God's glory is shown here on earth. Glorious!

Let's talk to God!

MY JOURNAL (choose one)

I think about you and praise you when I see these outrageously beautiful plants and animals you have made:

_____

_____

_____

_____

God, sometimes I don't feel very beautiful (on the inside). Help me to reflect you in this area of my life:

_____

_____

_____

_____

MY PRAYER

Lord, thank you for showing me your glory in the plants, animals, and even insects you have created. I want to be more beautiful in your eyes every day as I study your Word and get to know you better.

Butterflies are not born with wings. They begin life as caterpillars, climbing around leaves on sixteen or so suction cups at the end of stubby legs. When butterflies are in their caterpillar stage, their skin doesn't grow! As a caterpillar chomps on your mom's petunia plant, it grows, but it grows *out* of its skin. Like all insects, the caterpillar grows new skin underneath the old stuff and sheds its old skin. It just leaves it lying around and runs off to eat more tasty leaves. It may leave five to ten shells of its former self all over the place before it settles down to become a butterfly.

Just like caterpillars that shed their skin, God helps us grow out of our old, bad habits. When we decide that we want to be more like Christ, we get uncomfortable with our old ways and our old sins. Jesus can help us drop off those sins. It's like getting rid of an old layer of skin and putting on a new one that's more like Christ himself.

Think about what God says to you

Those who become Christians become new persons.
They are not the same anymore, for the old life is gone.
A new life has begun!

2 CORINTHIANS 5:17

In the above verse God talks to us through Paul, who wrote a lot of the New Testament. The new life that begins when Christ becomes the center of our lives can keep on being renewed over and over again. How? In Colossians 3:9-10 Paul writes, "Don't lie to each other, for you have stripped off your old evil nature and all its wicked deeds. In its place you have clothed yourselves with a brand-new nature that is continually being renewed as you learn more and more about Christ."

As life goes on, we can keep dropping off the old hide. Hey! Drop off one of those nasty old habits and grow into a new and better caterpillar!

Let's talk to God!

MY JOURNAL (choose one)

God, this is something that I have been angry about. I know it is part of my "old skin" that you want to take away. Give me your wisdom about how to handle this so that I can have your peace and no longer feel angry:

_____

_____

_____

_____

_____

God, this is an area in my life where I need your help to be less selfish,
less jealous, or more honest:

_____

_____

_____

_____

MY PRAYER

God, please help me to get rid of my old skin of impatience, anger, and
anything else that holds me down. I know you want me to be free of
these things so I can become more like you and have a good life. Thank
you for loving me enough to free me from that old, wrinkly skin!

The spot on this butterfly's wing looks like a big eye. (Photo courtesy Bill Gerrish)

Butterflies come in all shapes and sizes. The Queen Alexandra birdwing butterfly in New Guinea is eleven inches across. That's as big as a dinner plate! Then there are tiny ones like the dwarf blue. It's so small that it would fit on a penny with room to spare. And there is everything in between—big and small, bright and dull.

Each kind of butterfly is unique, with different patterns on its wings, different places to live, and different lifestyles. Butterflies live all over the world, from mountains to deserts to the tropical forests. Some of them even migrate like birds, cruising thousands of miles to their summer hideouts. It may sound like a "mission: impossible" for these delicate creatures to travel so far using their fragile wings, but God has uniquely designed them to be able to carry out their mission.

Just as God made each kind of butterfly unique, with its own mission, he made you unique too. God designed your body to look like it does. He has special places where he wants you to be, and he has given you specific interests and talents. God has known you from before the beginning, and he has made you for a mission on Earth. Perhaps it is to influence your friends or to help someone that nobody else will help. You might think of it as a "mission: impossible," but you are custom-made by your Creator-God, and he has wonderful plans for you!

Think about what God says to you

"For I know the plans I have for you," says the Lord.
*"They are plans for good and not for disaster,
to give you a future and a hope."*

JEREMIAH 29: 11

God's plans for us are greater than our own plans could ever be.
They may seem impossible to us, but nothing is impossible with God.
Because he is the Creator of all that exists, he knows just what all of
his creations are capable of doing. And he has the power to help us
follow through on the plans he has for us.

Let's talk to God!

MY JOURNAL (choose one)

*God, sometimes I feel as if I don't have anything to offer the world, but I
know that's not true. Here is a list of some things about me that you
have made special:*

_____

_____

_____

_____

God, this is something that seems like a "mission: impossible" to me. Help me see a way through this:

_____

_____

_____

_____

MY PRAYER

Thank you for making me special, God. Sometimes I don't feel very special, though. In those times, please help me to remember that you love me and that you have a mission for me that only I can do. Help me to understand that you really did put me here for a reason, and that you will always be here to help me.

DAY 4: In Disguise

These butterflies have wings that look like bark. This protects them as they hide on branches or in piles of dead leaves. (Photo courtesy Bill Gerrish)

Like they say in spy videos, "Things aren't always what they seem to be." That's true, even in the world of insects.

Caterpillars and butterflies wear some pretty crazy disguises to protect themselves. While most butterflies are bright and beautiful, some look like dead leaves sitting on a branch. What bird would be interested in eating a dried-up leaf? Many caterpillars and butterflies have big spots that look like scary eyes. There is even a butterfly that opens up its wings to look like an owl—and *nobody* wants to fool with an owl! Orange and black monarch butterflies taste bad to birds, and viceroy butterflies wear copycat orange and black colors and stripes. This protects them from any bird that has gagged on a monarch.

To birds, most caterpillars look like lunch. But some caterpillars go as far as to look like bird droppings so they won't get chewed! The juicy swallowtail caterpillars use stink warfare to keep foes away. You could say that they are the skunks of the insect world! A Y-shaped fork in their heads unleashes a gross smell. This fork is called an *osmeterium*. (Remember that word—you can use it to impress your friends at school!)

You can't judge a book by its cover or a caterpillar by its spots, stripes, or odor. But often we humans do this very thing. We decide we don't like people because of the kind of jeans they wear or the way they cut their hair or how small their muscles are. We decide— even before we talk to a person—that one of them is too old to be interesting and another is too different to get to know.

God cares about who we are, not how we look. Paul knew that this is true, for he was a little man with an unimpressive voice. But

God cared enough about him to make him one of the world's most famous missionaries.

Think about what God says to you

People judge by outward appearance, but the Lord looks at a person's thoughts and intentions.

1 SAMUEL 16:7

On his own, Samuel would never have chosen David, the youngest of many strong, good-looking brothers, to be the next king. But God's advice to Samuel was to look at what David was like on the inside— his thoughts and intentions. It's so easy to write people off without ever getting to know what they are really like. One good way to get "below the surface" with people is to just start talking to them. Ask them what they like to do and what they think about things. You may find out that you have a lot in common with them after all!

Let's talk to God!

MY JOURNAL (choose one)

Lord, this is someone I don't think is "cool" enough to be my friend. Help me to see him or her the way you do:

_____

_____

_____

_____

Lord, I know some kids don't think I'm "cool" enough to be their friend.
This is what it feels like to me:

_____

_____

_____

_____

MY PRAYER

Lord, help me to look at people and things the way you do. Help me to see beyond the way others appear and to look for the good in everyone, no matter how different I may think they look on the outside. Whatever a person wears or looks like, everyone is your creation!

Light shines through the colorful wings of this butterfly. (Photo courtesy Bill Gerrish)

More than any other creature, the butterfly is a symbol of Christianity. In paintings done by religious artists after the Middle Ages, you can find scenes of people doing normal things like going for a walk or working in a kitchen. But even in the indoor scenes, you find butterflies. They are sitting in a corner or hidden in the reflection of a vase. Pretty weird, right? But the artist put them there to show that no matter what was going on in the picture, the power of Jesus' resurrection was there too.

Think about why the butterfly symbolizes the power of Christ's rising from the grave. Just as Christ seemed to be dead and buried, a caterpillar hides itself in a cocoon (called a chrysalis) and seems to die. It no longer crawls around or eats. It just sleeps inside its organic "sleeping bag." Then, when it seems as if all is lost, the hard chrysalis begins to shake and move, and a butterfly breaks out—reborn! What once had suction cups and wrinkly skin now has beautiful wings to fly away. It's like Easter all over again.

Jesus was in a tomb until the third day. His disciples and other friends knew he was dead. They had seen him crucified on a cross, and the Romans had "finished him off" by jabbing a spear into his side. But on Easter morning, the power of the Spirit of God rolled a stone away from the tomb—a stone that undoubtedly weighed over a ton. But that was nothing compared to what was next: Jesus, dead in the tomb, rose again. Jesus was alive and he had defeated death! That's what we're reminded of when God gives a caterpillar wings to fly.

When we finally realize that Christ is "The Man," and that he has power over the universe, we also realize that we should give him control and care of our own lives. The moment we do that, the power of God makes us into a new being, a spiritual butterfly. We burst out of the chrysalis of our old ways and make a break for it! Our new life is not problem-free, but we have power to go through it and to do so with new joy. We're like a caterpillar that seems to come back from the dead, hatching into a creature with a radically new design. God's power gives us a new and better way of life.

Think about what God says to you

And just as Christ was raised from the dead by the glorious power of the Father, now we also may live new lives.

ROMANS 6:4

The start of something new is always exciting and a little scary: the first day of school, the first time you jump off a diving board, the first time you baby-sit. It's like that with our new life in Christ, too. It's exciting to think about bursting out of that chrysalis and starting a new life, but it also may feel a little weird. After all, we're pretty comfortable with the way we are, and we're not always sure how all these changes will feel. It's a pretty big adventure, but if you try it, you'll find it's worth it!

Let's talk to God!

MY JOURNAL (choose one)

When I think about my new life with you I get very excited about:

_____

_____

_____

_____

This is something I'm going to ask someone to help me understand about this "new life in Christ" thing:

_____

_____

_____

_____

MY PRAYER

Thank you, God, for sending Jesus to break me out of my "chrysalis." Help me to fly through life with his joy and power!

ACTIVITY IDEAS FOR WEEK 6

Hidden Pictures

Turn to the opening painting for Week 6. Hidden in the illustration are pictures of butterflies. How many can you find?

Butterfly Crossword Puzzle

Across

2. Who made the butterflies?
4. I shed my skin several times before I'm ready to be a butterfly
5. "King of butterflies"
6. A butterfly tastes with these
8. Butterflies smell with this

Down

1. A colorful winged insect
3. The tiniest butterfly
4. A caterpillar's cocoon
7. A butterfly's clear wings are covered with these

(Answers: Across—2. God; 4. caterpillar; 5. monarch; 6. feet; 8. antenna. Down—1. butterfly; 3. dwarf; 4. chrysalis; 7. scales.)

the human BODY

Thank you for making me
so wonderfully complex!
Your workmanship is marvelous—
and how well I know it.

PSALM 139:14

**LANDSCAPE OF THE INSIDE
OF THE HEART**
*A magical forest of muscle
and tendons guards the
entrance to the heart. Fresh
blood from the lungs pours
through this valve, which is
open in this view, and into
the left ventricle beyond.*

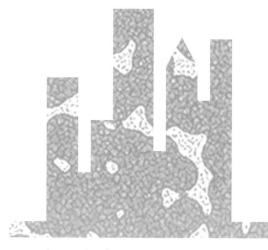

Your body is made of cells—lots of cells. In fact, a human body has a hundred times more cells than there are stars in our galaxy. We have different kinds of cells, including bone cells, eye cells, and blood cells. As they wear out, they are replaced by new ones. You may think your skin has been around for a while, but each of your skin cells lasts only about two weeks before it dies and falls off, and a new one takes its place. Bones seem as hard as stone, but the cells in your skeleton constantly dissolve. New bone cells are cranked out to replace old ones wherever your bones need to be stronger.

It's been three hundred years since Antonie van Leeuwenhoek invented a microscope. He saw microscopic beasts of all kinds, and he was probably the very first to see a real cell. He saw it as he looked at the blood of a frog. His sketches of cells show a dot in the middle of each one. He didn't realize how important that little dot was. It was the nucleus, or control center, of the cell. Each of your zillions of cells has one, and it contains that DNA map we saw in Week 5. Around the nucleus is a jelly-like blob called *cytoplasm,* where all the organelles (cell organs) float. It's all held together in a bag called the *membrane.*

The cells of the body are like the people in a city. They all rely upon each other to make a total community. Cells communicate with each other; they pass food and waste from one to another; and when one dies, the others "clean" it up. Scientists can't study cells inside someone's body very well, so sometimes they take a cell out and put it in a jar where the cell *thinks* it is in a body. But most cells cannot live for long without their neighbors. They are designed to live as part of a group.

God designed the cells in our body to work together and help each other. In the same way, he designed people to work together and help each other in the "church body." We need Christian friends to work with, play with, and share our thoughts and dreams and hopes with.

Think about what God says to you

We will hold to the truth in love, becoming more and more in every way like Christ, who is the head of his body, the church. Under his direction, the whole body is fitted together perfectly. As each part does its own special work, it helps the other parts grow, so that the whole body is healthy and growing and full of love.

EPHESIANS 4:15-16

Our God is a God of relationships. He has created us so that we function best when we are part of a larger community of believers. Without these special relationships we lose our spiritual energy, much like a cell does when it is separated from the body. Just think about how special your Christian friends are—you can work and play with them, as well as share your thoughts, dreams, and hopes with them. And together you will grow in your love for Jesus and one another.

Let's talk to God!

MY JOURNAL (choose one)

This is why I think you want us to get together as a community to serve and worship you:

_____

_____

_____

_____

This is what might happen to my relationship with you if I would stop worshiping with other Christians or spending time with them:

_____

_____

_____

_____

MY PRAYER
Thank you for giving me a group of believers to worship with and serve you with. Help me to love all of the people in my church as if they were my own brothers and sisters, parents and grandparents.

Microscope Man

Antonie van Leeuwenhoek was a Dutchman who lived in the 1600s. He started life as a draper's apprentice and used a lens to study the weave of the cloth. This maybe gave him the idea for designing what may have been the very first microscope. He loved to study nature, and he looked at everything he could find under his microscopes, writing down and sketching what he saw. He saw single-celled creatures that we now call protozoa and named them "animalcules."

Would you like to try sketching some of the microscopic critters shown in the photos on page 72?

Our bodies are the vehicles that God has made to carry our souls around on Earth. They are designed so that we can be in contact with the physical world, even though the "real us" is inside these bodies.

Each of our five senses works in a different way to gather data about what's happening around us. This data is then zipped up to our brain through amazingly fast nerve pathways. Let's take a look at each of the five senses.

Vision: The eye is a ball filled with a kind of jelly. In front is an opening like the lens of a camera. Light goes through the hole, through the jelly, and hits the back of the eye. Back there are light sensors called rods, which see in black and white, and cones, which see in color. Rods are great for seeing in dim light. Many animals see only in black and white, so they can see well at night. We can see in color, but not well at night because the cones get in the way. Our eyes can see quick movement, and they can see color better than most cameras. Two eyes used at the same time can see in three dimensions, which helps us walk around without bumbling into each other. They are wonderful inventions!

Hearing: Our ears have a flap of skin inside called an eardrum. The eardrum vibrates when sound hits it. Our brain turns those vibrations into all the sounds we hear. Think how many different sounds our ears can handle: music, chirping birds, rumbling thunder, car horns, your parents calling "Dinner!" And you can tell the difference between people's voices, even on the phone.

Touch: Branchlike nerve cells all over our body let us feel hot and cold, sharp and dull, rough and smooth. Guess which two parts of your body have the most nerve receptors per square inch? Your fingers and your tongue!

Taste: The tongue is not only good at feeling things, but it can taste, too! It is covered with tiny bumps called taste buds. Each bud is specialized to identify one taste. A map of the tongue's taste buds would show the sweet and salt buds near the tip of the tongue, the sour buds on the sides, and the bitter buds at the back of the tongue.

Smell: Our nose clues us in on what's perfume and what's skunk. Our smell detectors are in the upper part of the nose.

Each part of our body has its own special job to do. But the parts also cooperate. Smell and taste work together to provide more data to the brain. If one of the senses is damaged or lost, the others work harder. In the same way, in our church we have our own special jobs and talents we can use. And we have to work harder when some don't do their part.

Think about what God says to you

God made our bodies with many parts, and he has put each part just where he wants it. What a strange thing a body would be if it had only one part! Yes, there are many parts, but only one body. The eye can never say to the hand, "I don't need you." The head can't say to the feet, "I don't need you." Now all of you together are Christ's body, and each one of you is a separate and necessary part of it.

1 CORINTHIANS 12:18-21, 27

In the Bible Paul reminds us that our bodies have many parts and all are important. He also tells us that all people who love Jesus ("all of you together") are part of one big body. This body is called "the church" or "Christ's body" or "God's family." In God's family all over the world, each of us has a special purpose—each of us is a necessary part of the church. (Remember that this refers to people, not just a building. If you believe in Jesus, you are part of the church around the world. You are also part of a local group of believers—a congregation that you call your church.)

What do you think your own special work in your church is? If you don't know, be patient! God will let you know by the opportunities he gives you to help others.

Let's talk to God!

MY JOURNAL (choose one)

If I sing in the kids' choir, I am being a "voice" in my local church body. Here is another "part" that I am:

_____

_____

_____

_____

This is a way my mom, dad, or friends serve in our church body:

_____

_____

_____

MY PRAYER

Thank you, God, for showing me that all Christians are part of Christ's body, the church. It's fun to think of all the different "parts" I can be as I grow up. Help me to remember that when I lovingly run an errand for someone, I am helping to be the "feet" of my church. And when I work with some of the younger kids on a Sunday school craft, I am the "hands."

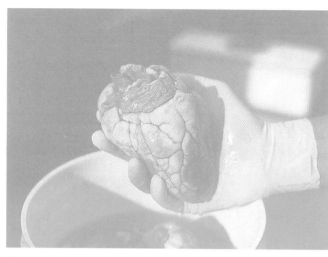

This sheep heart is about the same size and form as a human heart.

Plug up your ears. Do you hear it? Press your fingers against the side of your neck. Can you feel it? It's the beating of your heart, and it's sending gallons of blood through your body all the time. Your heart is the hardest working muscle in your whole body. As long as you are alive, it never stops working! It usually beats more than once a second. About seventy times per minute your heart pushes and pulls the blood through your vessels, sending oxygen and nutrients (tiny bits of food) to every part of your body. What an amazing organ!

If you hold both fists together you will see how big your heart is. Each heartbeat squeezes out about one-third cup of blood. Around eighteen hundred gallons of blood flow in and out of your heart each day! It all travels through the branching bunch of blood vessels in your body.

You have three kinds of blood vessels: *Arteries* carry "new" blood, full of oxygen and nutrients, away from the heart. *Capillaries,* the smallest blood vessels, release the oxygen and nutrients through their walls and into your body. *Veins* carry "used" blood back to the heart after its oxygen and nutrients have been used up. The heart then pumps this blood to your lungs, where it gets oxygen again and flows back to your heart. From there the blood is pushed out through the arteries and goes back through your body. The entire trip from your body to your heart, to your lungs, back to your heart, and then out again takes just twenty-five seconds. Pretty efficient machine, huh?

But when this efficient machine doesn't work right, the person who has the defective heart gets very sick. Sometimes they need a new heart. In 1967 Christiaan Barnard was the first doctor to successfully transplant a human heart.

But God has been doing "heart transplants" for much longer than that! He can take a heart that's spiritually sick with sin and replace it with a new heart.

Think about what God says to you

A good person produces good deeds from a good heart, and an evil person produces evil deeds from an evil heart. Whatever is in your heart determines what you say.

LUKE 6:45

No one can hide a sinful heart forever. Eventually the anger, jealousy, and other yucky stuff will come spilling out. In Psalm 51:10 King David said, "Create in me a clean heart, O God. Renew a right spirit within me." How clean and healthy is your heart? Have you invited God to clean up your heart so that the Holy Spirit can happily dwell there?

Let's talk to God!

MY JOURNAL (choose one)

Here is what I'm like when my heart is right with you:

_____

_____

_____

When my heart isn't right, this is what happens:

_____

_____

_____

_____

MY PRAYER

"Create in me a clean heart, O God." I want it to always produce good words and good actions so that people know I belong to you!

Way-Cool Blood Data

- If you could stretch out your blood vessels in a straight line, end to end, they would go around the world two and a half times.
- And how about this: Your blood is like salt water with red and white blood cells floating in it. In fact, 98 percent of your body is water.
- An adult has about 35 trillion blood cells.
- The life span of a blood cell is four months. During that time it makes 160,000 trips to and from the heart.

How Much Water?

Take a deck of playing cards and remove two cards. (If there are jokers, take them out too.) Place the remaining cards face down on the table in seven rows of seven cards each. Now place the extra card face up at the end of the last row. The one that is face up represents how much of your body is bone, skin, and other solid stuff. The rest of the cards are water!

DAY 4: YOUR BRAIN: DON'T LEAVE HOME WITHOUT IT!

A man with two brains: Biology professor Dr. Anil Rao has one brain in his hands and one in his head. (He says the one in his head works better.)

It's almost as big as your head. It looks like a pile of gray pudding. It's what you think with. It's your *brain!* Every thought you have, every feeling you feel, every action you take, is processed in your brain. It's the boss of your "bod," the supervisor of your earthly self, the director of your direction. Your brain is a complex computer in your head, and it can do more than any desktop PC. Wow!

While you are reading this page, you are using your cerebral cortex—the wrinkly part at the top of your brain—to think about and maybe even remember what you read! The cerebral cortex is part of your cerebrum. You use the cerebrum to reason, to make decisions, and to imagine. The cerebrum is split into two sides, or hemispheres. The left side of your cerebrum handles speaking and learning languages. The right side is more visual, judging distance and shape. This is the side that you use the most when you draw.

Under the cerebrum is the cerebellum. This gives you balance and makes your muscles work together.

At the bottom of your brain is the brain stem, which connects the brain to the spinal cord. It's like a switchboard operator, receiving messages from one part of your body and sending the messages to different parts of your brain. The brain stem collects data from the various systems in your body, telling you how warm or cold, thirsty or hungry, and tired or alert you are. It also keeps your heart and lungs moving automatically so you don't have to think about doing those things.

God gave you a brain to figure things out. When you sit down to read the Bible, or when you go to church, he doesn't want you to check your brain at the door. God likes questions. Ask him. He knows everything.

Think about what God says to you

This man Daniel ... has a sharp mind and is filled with divine knowledge and understanding.

DANIEL 5:12

God wants you to think carefully about what you are taught—even what you are taught by your Sunday school teachers. Does what they say agree with Scripture? If you really understand the basis of your faith in God, you will be able to explain it and discuss it with others. Are you able to do that?

Take some time to think about why you believe the way you do. But don't be nervous if someone asks you a question about God that you can't answer right away. And don't worry if you have a question that you can't find an answer to. The answers are there, in the Bible or in the wisdom of other godly people. Often God answers our questions by saying we should wait for a while or look again at the Bible. God wants us to use our minds to discuss things with each other and with him. Christianity is for thinking people!

Let's talk to God!

MY JOURNAL (choose one)

This is why I believe in you, God:

_____

_____

_____

This is what I used to think you are like, but now I understand better:

_____

_____

_____

_____

MY PRAYER

Lord, help me to use the brain power you gave me. I want to be able to think through my faith in you until I really own it. It's not just my parents' or my friend's faith—it's mine. Help me to ask hard questions and look for answers.

Many kinds of bacteria can make you sick. These microscopic critters are called *Actinomyces Viscosus T14V. (Photo courtesy Dr. Joan Foster)*

These bacteria can cause strep throat. Their scientific name i *Streptococcus Sanguis 34. (Photo courtesy Dr. Joan Foster)*

The world is full of microscopic creatures called germs. They are in the water and air. They get on our hands and even in our food. That's why it is so important to wash our hands after we use the rest room and before we eat. But no matter how careful we are, germs—bacteria and viruses—get inside us. Germs can cause colds, flu, and more serious diseases.

God has designed an army inside our bodies to battle incoming germs. A special kind of white blood cell called a *lymphocyte* makes the weapons for the war. These weapons are called *antibodies*.

An antibody is like a tiny Pac-Man that travels around in the blood in search of any bacteria it can munch up. Our bodies make thousands of different kinds of antibodies to protect us from many kinds of germs. When a germ that needs to be attacked comes into the body, the lymphocytes sound the alarm, and many antibodies are made. The war is on. We get stuffy noses or fevers, but the battle is being fought and won by the microscopic warriors. Sometimes the battle goes on for days, like when we get the flu. But once our bodies figure out how to make antibodies for a certain bacteria or virus, we probably won't get sick from it again.

There are some diseases that normal antibodies cannot combat.

Medical researchers try to develop medicines called *vaccines* to keep people from getting these diseases. Vaccines contain germs from a disease, but the germs have been made harmless. The body recognizes these germs and is fooled into making antibodies against the disease. The result is that we won't catch the disease even if we get some of its real germs. There are vaccines for many diseases that used to cripple or even kill people, such as polio and tuberculosis.

But what if you are already sick and your body needs help to win its fight against a disease? Scientists have discovered how to make antibiotics, which are drugs that are poisonous to bacteria. For example, penicillin, a drug made from mold, helps us to get over strep throat and bacterial pneumonia. There are many other drugs that help. Some drugs even kill viruses, but not the ones that cause colds. Our antibodies must be left to do that by themselves. AIDS is a very serious virus that destroys the immune system. There are no drugs to cure it yet. Fortunately, it is very difficult to get AIDS.

Is God the one who heals us, or is it the doctors? One of God's special names is Jehovah Rophe, which means "God our Healer." God designed our bodies to be able to fight off diseases, and he also gave scientists and doctors the wisdom to invent vaccines and antibiotics. So what do you think the answer is?

Think about what God says to you

I will give you back your health
and heal your wounds, says the Lord.
JEREMIAH 30:17

When God created our world, it was free of sickness, pain, and death. But when Adam and Eve sinned in the Garden of Eden, sickness and death entered the world. Even so, God still can and does heal illnesses.

Let's talk to God!

MY JOURNAL (choose one)

Lord, I want to ask you to heal this person:

_____

_____

_____

_____

Thank you for helping in all of these ways when I am sick:

_____

_____

_____

_____

MY PRAYER

Lord, I praise you for being Jehovah Rophe, our Healer.

Word Scramble

Unscramble the following words from this week's lessons:

1. irsoepcocm
2. nsoetlek
3. neyogx
4. aierctab
5. airnb

(Answers: 1. microscope; 2. skeleton; 3. oxygen; 4. bacteria; 5. brain)

LIFESTYLES
of the big and fossilized

So God created great sea creatures and every sort of fish and every kind of bird. And God saw that it was good.

GENESIS 1:21

TYRANNOSAURUS HUNT IN ALASKA
Fossils show that Tyrannosaurus Rex lived and hunted in Alaska, where the winter nights were very long. T-Rex may have been able to see well in the dark.

DAY 1: ONE WHALE OF A SHALE

A peculiar creature called *Anomalocaris* was the worst monster of the Burgess Shale zoo. With teeth like a can opener and fierce claws, this three-foot-long bully probably had a hard time eating the spined *Hallucigenia* (on sand at right) but may ha[ve] munched on the tuliplike animal, *Dinomiscus* (left).

There are monsters in Canada. They are waiting up there in the mountains with googly-eyed stalks for bodies, with plates and spines, with claws and stingers, and with mouths built like blenders. But before you worry too much about becoming someone's lunch in the Canadian Rockies, remind yourself that these beasts haven't eaten for a very long time, and they aren't going anywhere. They are frozen in time, turned to stone within the rocks of the mysterious Burgess Shale.

The Burgess Shale is a rocky outcropping in British Columbia. Shale is a claylike rock that breaks into thin layers. It used to be under water, part of an ancient sea that is now long gone, but it left us fossils of many of its tenants. These creatures are so weird that nobody understood what they really looked like for many years. Scientists tried to match the fossils with recognizable living things: was that a shrimp? a worm? a crab? They made drawings of the way they thought things looked before they became fossils, but most of their ideas were way off. What they thought was a headless shrimp was actually the clawed arm of a "bizarro" beastie named *Anomalocaris*. This is one you would see in

Trilobites like these lived with other creatures in the lagoon that became the Burgess Shale. Notice their ribbed, three-part bodies and huge eyes.

your dreams—or nightmares. It had a round mouth of jagged teeth that probably would have made a good can opener. Another oddball was the *Dinomiscus,* a tulip-shaped animal that anchored itself in the sand and waved in the water. There were other leaflike crawlies, things that looked more like flowers than animals, and worms with tentacles.

Life was dangerous in the Burgess Shale. All those animals with all those teeth! Many animals were decked out in elegant armor for protection. The wormy *Hallucigenia* had two rows of spines along its back. The *Halkierid* looked like a slug with chain mail and a little flat helmet on each end. The *Wiwaxia* carried armor to the extreme, with interlocking plates and spikes to keep hungry eaters away.

Creatures of the Burgess Shale were armored against big things with even bigger teeth. God has given us armor for protection too—not against chompers, but against spiritual battles that we must fight.

Think about what God says to you

Stand your ground, putting on the sturdy belt of truth and the body armor of God's righteousness. For shoes, put on the peace that comes from the Good News, so that you will be fully prepared. In every battle you will need faith as your shield to stop the fiery arrows aimed at you by Satan. Put on salvation as your helmet, and take the sword of the Spirit, which is the Word of God.

EPHESIANS 6:14-17

In the verses above, Paul reminds Christians to put on the full armor of God. When Satan tempts us, we need to be protected from head to foot:

- If you have asked Jesus to be your Savior, you have the helmet of *salvation* on your head.
- If you regularly read God's words of truth in the *Bible,* it's like fighting Satan's lies with a sword.
- If you believe God's *truth,* it's like wearing a belt that holds you together.
- If you have *faith* that God has the power to help you, it's as if you have a shield to keep you safe. You'll be safe from the doubts and fears that Satan wants to put in your mind. And you'll have God's strength to stay away from all that's evil.
- If you understand that you can never be totally good and righteous— only God can—it's as if you are completely covered with the armor of *God's goodness.* Satan can't get through anywhere!
- Then, if you believe that Jesus really came to be the Savior of the world, from the top of your head way down to your shoes, you'll have God's *peace.* And your shoes will take you to share that peace with everyone around you.

Ask your mom or dad to pray with you every morning before you go to school. It's a good idea to pray the verses from Ephesians 6 so you will be reminded that God gives you the tools you need to be out there in the wild world!

Let's talk to God!

MY JOURNAL

God, this is the one piece of armor that I will probably need the most today:

_____

_____

MY PRAYER

Lord, I thank you for giving me the belt of truth, the armor of your righteousness, the shoes of the gospel of peace, the shield of faith, the helmet of salvation, and the sword of the Spirit. Satan's fiery arrows can't get me as long as I remember to "dress for battle" every day.

Stegosaurus *is chased by an* Allosaurus. *Will her plates and tail spikes save her? Since this painting was done, scientists have discovered that the spikes stuck out of the sides of the tail rather than the top.*

In the time leading up to the creation of humans, God populated Earth with a riotous parade of living things. These included weird sea animals with eyes on their arms, plated crab-creatures with feelers and three blobby eyes, gooey things with no eyes but lots of legs, and eventually, the dinosaurs.

Dinosaurs came in all sizes, shapes, and colors. The biggest dinosaur that has been dug up so far is a gentle plant eater called *Seismosaur,* 120 feet long. This graceful giant had a swanlike neck (its neck bones are a lot like bird neck bones) and a tail-like whip. It walked on four elephantlike legs but could lean back on its rear legs, balancing on its tail to reach the tallest trees.

Seismosaur had company. Many creatures looked very similar to *Seismosaur,* and they fall into a group called *sauropods.* They include such strange critters as *Ultrasauros, Supersaurus, Brachiosaurus, Apatosaurus* (which used to be called *Brontosaurus*), and *Diplodocus.* These dinosaurs appear to have cared for their young and to hang out together in groups.

God designed these long-necked leaf eaters so they could see over trees and spot danger coming. Some scientists now believe that sauropods could rear up in the air and even use their tails to make a loud *crack!* just like a bullwhip to warn the herd of danger and even scare off their enemies.

Because of their long necks, the sauropods had a nice, high view of their world and could see far distances. In the same way that God provided these dinosaurs with long necks so they could see far away, he has provided us with his Word, the Bible, to help us see far away and to give us a "heavenly viewpoint" of our world.

Think about what God says to you

We don't look at the troubles we can see right now; rather, we look forward to what we have not yet seen. For the troubles we see will soon be over, but the joys to come will last forever.

2 CORINTHIANS 4:18

God in his Word reminds you from his heavenly viewpoint that Jesus is coming again. Watch for him! God wants you to know that your life is eternal. Plan on it! Heaven is a wonderful place—there will be no troubles, only joys that "will last forever." Look forward to it!

Let's talk to God!

MY JOURNAL

God, here are some things your Word shows me that "help me see things" from your point of view:

_____

_____

_____

_____

MY PRAYER

Lord, I want to spend time reading your Word and learning more about how you see things. Then, like the sauropods, which could look past the trees, when times get hard I can look past my troubles and look forward to the good stuff.

A herd of Triceratops runs from a wildfire sparked by a thunderstorm.

Check out the duds, dude! Those dinosaurs were decked "to the max." Some had horns and helmets. Others had spikes and armored plates. Paleontologists (people who study creatures that lived long, long ago) believe many dinosaurs may have been as colorful as tropical birds, with superb splotches, dazzling dots, and sassy stripes. A favorite type was the *Triceratops,* a triple-horned beast as big as an elephant. *Triceratops* had a collar sprouting from the back of his head. Although he weighed up to five tons, his strong legs were made for galloping, probably much like a rhinoceros.

Another fine-fashioned "phenom" was the *Stegosaurus.* This weirdly cool vegetarian wore a double row of pointed plates on his back. The plates made munching on him a bit tricky for the meat eaters like *Allosaurus.* The plates may also have been used to keep cool. Elephants wave their ears in the breeze, and *Stegosaurus* may have done the same with his plates. If *Stegosaurus* was attacked, he had a few tricks besides those pretty plates. His throat was armored with stony scales, and he had four nasty spikes on the end of his tail. These made a nifty weapon.

There were other armored *amigos,* including the multi-horned *Styracosaurus,* the extremely crowned *Chasmosaurus,* and crested wonders like *Corythosaurus* and the duck-billed *Hypacrosaurus.*

Ankylosaurs had clubbed tails and *Nodosaurs* had spiked sides. All of these body decorations were useful—some for defense, some for displays, and some for making noise. Crowns on the tops of heads helped creatures chirp, growl, and bugle. The world of the dinosaurs was spectacular in sight and sound. Those cool creatures knew how to strut their stuff!

Do you have any idea how beautiful you are to God? He decorated those crazy dinosaurs, which didn't even have a soul, to be ravishing. But he made you in his very own image, much more beautiful than any dinosaur ever was.

Think about what God says to you

*You should be known for the beauty that comes from within,
the unfading beauty of a gentle and quiet spirit,
which is so precious to God.*

1 PETER 3:4

When you understand how truly beautiful you are to God—how precious, special, and unique—you can relax and enjoy life. And the really cool part is that then others will be attracted to you, because they will see something unusual and wonderful. They will want to find out what it is that makes you different. And you'll get to tell them the answer: God!

Let's talk to God!

MY JOURNAL

God, these are some special ways you have made me beautiful to you:

_____

_____

_____

_____

MY PRAYER

Lord, I don't really understand how beautiful I am in your sight. Help me to understand better, and to enjoy the security and peace that comes from knowing that you created me to be beautiful and special in your image.

DAY 4: DINOSAUR FATHEAD

This fossilized Tyrannosaurus rex *bares his five-inch-long teeth. Notice the knifelike edges. (Photo courtesy Denver Museum of Natural History)*

Tyrannosaurus rex was one of the biggest, most terrifying creatures ever to roam Earth. From the edge of his square nose to the point of his powerful tail, he was forty-five feet long. He had a gigantic head compared to the rest of his body, and that head was split by a scary mouth with teeth five inches long. Cavities would not have been good for *T. rex.*

The skull of this colossal character had large places for the eyes, which makes some scientists think the creature had excellent night vision. Some *T. rexes* have been found in Alaska, where there were very long, dark nights. This would mean that he may have been a nocturnal predator.

Because his head was so long, *T. rex* had to lose some pounds somewhere else. He had mini-arms, but they were powerful, with sharp claws. Those small arms could lift six hundred pounds.

For a long time there were only three tyrannosaur skeletons in the entire world. People used to think that *T. rex* was a slow, lumbering thug with nearly useless forearms, and that he ate dead meat. But as more skeletons have been found, our view of this king of terror has changed. *T. rex* was fast and strong. His front arms were powerful weapons, and his slashing teeth and large eyes made him a great hunter. *T. rex* was a killing machine. His strong legs could send him "jammin'" after lunch much faster than most of his prey could go. But did *T. rex* always win? Did he always catch his prey? No, there were some great battles and great escapes. *Triceratops* was smaller than *T. rex*, but he was well armored, and a worthy opponent. When attacked, he could gore and gouge *T. rex* with his three-foot-long horns!

Satan (also known as the Devil) is one mean predator. He may try to make us think that we're not good enough to follow Jesus. He may remind us that we did something wrong once and make us feel that it won't matter if we do it again. He may try to convince us that everyone else is "doing it," so why should we want to be different? He may even try to make us believe that there is no such thing as right or wrong. But does Satan have to win in our lives? *No!* We just need to be prepared and on our guard. We need to fight Satan with our spiritual armor, remembering that those weapons will never fail.

Think about what God says to you

Be careful! Watch out for attacks from the Devil, your great enemy. He prowls around like a roaring lion, looking for some victim to devour. Take a firm stand against him, and be strong in your faith.

1 PETER 5:8-9

God gives you all the weapons you need to battle Satan, including salvation, faith, truth, and the Bible. (You may want to look again at Day 1 to review the list from Ephesians 6:14-17.) If you trust Jesus, you'll never have to fight Satan alone. Jesus said, "I have overcome the world" (John 16:33). That includes the power of Satan in this world. With Jesus' help, you'll be able to "resist the Devil, and he will flee from you" (James 4:7). Not even Satan can separate us from the love of Jesus Christ. "Overwhelming victory is ours through Christ, who loved us" (Romans 8:37).

Grab some weapons today!

Let's talk to God!

MY JOURNAL (choose one)

God, this is a good verse I can use to fight off Satan when he attacks with his lies:

_____

_____

_____

_____

Here is one lie Satan has used to attack me with:

_____

_____

_____

MY PRAYER

Lord, your Word says, "Resist the Devil, and he will flee from you." Help me not to wander around unprepared, but to stand firm in my faith and be ready to fight Satan off with your Word when he attacks me with his lies.

Stegosaurus *had a row of plates on his back to protect him. This plate is on the back of a* Stegosaurus *found in Colorado. (Photo courtesy Denver Museum of Natural History)*

If you look around at the animal kingdom today, you will quickly notice one thing: There aren't any more dinosaurs. There used to be lots of them. They were strong and fast, and some were probably pretty smart.

When we think of the ancient life-forms that are gone, we wonder what they were really like. We feel a sense of loss that these strange and wonderful creatures are gone forever (unless someone invents a Jurassic Park). But what if one of these ancient creatures did come back?

For many years, paleontologists found fossils of an ancient five-foot-long fish called a *coelacanth* (SEE-luh-kanth). This teenage mutant ninja tuna had armlike flippers for fins, a three-lobed tail, and sharp spines. Its body was armored like many of the later dinosaurs, and it lived in ancient seas now long gone.

Scientists assumed the coelacanth had gone the way of the dinosaur, lost forever, another extinct creature of the past. Then, in 1938, a fisherman caught a living one in deep waters off the coast of South Africa. Fossil hunters were "jazzed, pumped"— ecstatic! Here was a living fossil, a life-form that was once thought to be gone but now was found alive and kicking (well, swimming). Since that time many coelacanths have been found living in the deep, dark waters near Madagascar.

What an amazing thing it was for people to see a beautiful, strange creature alive and well after having found all those fossils. It was a dream come true for many fossil-fish fans, and for agile anglers (fishermen), too.

Jesus told a story about someone who was lost and then found again. It's often called the story of the "Prodigal Son," but the tale is about the father, too. You probably remember the story. A young man leaves home to explore the world, wastes all of his money and becomes poor, and finally returns home. His father, who is waiting for him, is so happy to see his son that he throws a welcome-home party. This is the way God feels when we turn to him. We might try running our lives our own way, ignoring God until we get into trouble. But even after we have been foolish, when we turn to our Father in heaven, he is happier than a paleontologist with a coelacanth!

Think about what God says to you

Your brother was dead and has come back to life!
He was lost, but now he is found!
LUKE 15:32

One of the reasons why Jesus told this story was to show how God rejoices when each of us turns to him. It's a strange head-bender to think that the infinite, incredibly powerful Creator of all things would even care about us. But we actually bring delight to God when we lean on him in times of trouble, when we call to him in times of decision-making, and when we soar through life on the "big-daddy" wave of joy that only our Father in heaven can bring.

Let's talk to God!

MY JOURNAL (choose one)

Lord, here is an area of my life where I need to come back to you:

_____

_____

_____

_____

God, this is someone I know who is like the Prodigal Son. Show me how to help this person come back to you:

_____

_____

_____

_____

MY PRAYER

God, help me to not be a "Prodigal" son or daughter to you. Thank you that you have always loved me and that no matter what I do, you don't love me more or less. Help me to remember that I can bring joy to you—the great, vast, and awesome Creator—by hanging in there with you in good times and bad.

Fossilized Funny Bones
Q: What do you call dinosaur car crashes?
A: Tyrannosaurus wrecks.

Q: What dinosaur has three horns and three wheels?
A: Tri-cycle-tops.

Q: Why is *Stegosaurus* a good dinner guest?
A: She always brings her own plates.

Q: What ancient animals always lied?
A: Am-FIB-ians.

Dino Web Sites
Here are some fun Web sites. Check them out to learn more about dinosaurs:

1. www.ZoomSchool.com/subjects/dinosaurs

2. http://cotf.edu/ete/modules/msese/dinosaur.html

3. www.isgs.uiuc.edu/isgsroot/dinos/home.html
   (Dino Russ's Lair)

SHAKIN'
and
QUAKIN'

Moses led [the people] out from the camp to meet with God, and they stood at the foot of the mountain. All Mount Sinai was covered with smoke because the Lord had descended on it in the form of fire. The smoke billowed into the sky like smoke from a furnace, and the whole mountain shook with a violent earthquake.

EXODUS 19:17-18

Powerful forces such as volcanoes have sculpted our world into the "jammin'" place it is today

God has used earthquakes, volcanoes, and even meteors to make Earth into the "jammin'" place it is today.

In Week 2 (Home Sweet Home) we saw that Earth is a jigsaw planet. Its crust is fractured into pieces that float on a sea of hot, partly molten rock. As these pieces called tectonic plates float around, they push against each other, causing friction. That's when the excitement begins.

At the edge of these plates, the rock heats up and we get volcanoes and earthquakes.

About half a million earthquakes shake up our world each year. Most are caused by the rumbling of volcanoes, the rattling of landslides, or the collapse of underground caves. These quakes are felt only by people nearby, and they are usually gentle.

But some earthquakes are much more powerful and are caused by the movement of the earth's plates. When two plates grind together or ram into each other, the movement is usually so gradual that we don't feel it. Over long periods, mountains rise and rocks move. But every once in a while the plates get stuck. Pressure builds up until they slip again. This slip is felt as a jerk deep in the ground, which we call an earthquake. The abrupt movement of the plates sends a shock wave through miles and miles of ground. This kind of earthquake can last for seconds or minutes.

These earthquakes are often deadly. The worst recorded earthquake of all time happened in Shensi Province, China, in 1556. Eight hundred thousand people died. The city of San Francisco was nearly destroyed by an earthquake and fire in 1906. In Kobe, Japan, highways were overturned, buildings were crumbled, and over five thousand people were killed when the earth shook in 1995.

When an earthquake happens on the sea floor, the shock can cause a gigantic wave, called a tidal wave or *tsunami*. Often a tsunami does more damage than the earthquake that caused it.

Earthquakes, floods, and fires remind us of our need for the God who is bigger than any disaster. It's hard to understand why scary things happen. But if they didn't, we wouldn't need to trust in God. We wouldn't need faith in him if our world was completely gentle and safe. So remember: Bad things sometimes happen, but God is in control.

Think about what God says to you

God is our refuge and strength, always ready to help in times of trouble. So we will not fear, even if earthquakes come and the mountains crumble into the sea.

PSALM 46:1-2

When you think about all the natural disasters that could happen, it's easy to get scared. But who gives the spirit of fear? Satan. "For God has not given us a spirit of fear and timidity, but of power." (2 Timothy 1:7). God is in charge of everything. He has the power to help you through any kind of trouble, and he wants you to know that he will always be there for you. You can trust him even when there's a "whole lot of shakin' goin' on!"

Let's talk to God!

MY JOURNAL

God, there isn't a real earthquake out there right now, but this is something in my life that is "shakin' me up," and I need to tell you about it:

_____

_____

_____

_____

MY PRAYER:

Lord, I will trust you as my hiding place and my protector when frightening things are going on all around me. You are much bigger than any bad thing that could ever happen.

Earthquakes in the Bible

Earthquakes show us the phenomenal power God has put into this planet. Even though they can cause great hardship, God uses earthquakes as a tool for his plan.

Look up the following verses in your Bible and write down some ways that God has used earthquakes:

Matthew 27:51-54

_____

Matthew 28:1-7

_____

Acts 16:25-32

_____

DAY 2: VOLCANO: A MOUNTAIN THAT BLOWS ITS TOP

Two great forces of nature meet as the Grímsvötn volcano breaks through the glacier Vatnajökull. (Photo courtesy Magnus Tumi Gudmundson)

A hundred years ago the famous novelist Jules Verne wrote a book called *Journey to the Center of the Earth.* This exciting adventure tells of some explorers who climbed down the throat of a sleeping volcano in Iceland to trek to the center of the earth. (Hmm, wonder how he got the title?)

What's wrong with this picture? In Verne's time some people thought the earth might be hollow, with caverns that wandered all the way through the middle. We now know that just below the earth's thin crust, there is liquid rock that's hot enough to melt metal! Verne's trip would not have been fun unless he had an overcoat made of titanium!

Why is the earth's core so hot? Leftover heat from the creation of our world provides some of it, but most of the heat comes from radioactive material in the earth's crust. Radioactive rock keeps things

Craters of volcanoes steam in one of Iceland's most volcanic regions, Mývatn.

melted and toasty down there. Pressure builds up until the heat wants to escape. Finally, so much pressure builds up that heat and melted rock (lava) gush up through a weak spot in the earth's crust, often along the edges of those plates we talked about earlier this week. And there you have it—a *volcano!*

This lava is called Pahoehoe, *a Hawaiian word describing a type of lava with a smooth, shiny surface.*

Volcanoes build beautiful mountains with rich soil for farming. The problem is that this rich soil is dangerously close to the volcano. So the next time a big eruption occurs, what happens? No more farmland, houses, or people!

One such volcano blew its stack

seventy-nine years after the birth of Christ. Mount Vesuvius had been smoking and making earthquakes for a long time, and the people in the nearby Italian village of Pompeii kept a nervous eye on the great mountain. One day Vesuvius exploded. Ashes and stones fell from the sky, burying the entire village and many of its people. When "Indiana Jones" types started digging around sixteen centuries later, they found that there were empty places in the ash where things had dissolved. They poured plaster into the holes and made perfect statues of Pompeiian people frozen in the lava for all to see. Two Pompeiians were caught sleeping when the ash came. Another was sitting with her dog, and a father was found protecting his child.

None of these people could have imagined that two thousand years later we would be able to see what they had been doing when the volcano erupted. If they had known that other people would be looking at them someday, how glad they would have been that they weren't doing anything embarrassing! In the same way, we need to remember that God sees everything we do and knows about everything we say or even think.

Think about what God says to you

The time is coming when everything will be revealed; all that is secret will be made public. Whatever you have said in the dark will be heard in the light, and what you have whispered behind closed doors will be shouted from the housetops for all to hear!
Luke 12:2-3

Someday everyone will be able to see other people's secret sins. Yikes! That will be a red-faced day for lots of people. But how happy everyone will be whose Savior is Jesus. When he forgives our sins, he doesn't cover us with plaster and put us on display—he takes our sins away (see 1 John 2:1-2). So who will condemn us? Neither God the Father nor his Son, Jesus, for Jesus died to save us and now sits right next to God, "pleading for us" (see Romans 8:33-34). God promises, "I will forgive their wrongdoings, and I will never again remember their sins" (Hebrews 8:12).

Let's talk to God!

MY JOURNAL (choose one)

God, this is how I feel when I try to keep a secret from you:

_____

_____

_____

_____

God, this is how I feel when I tell your Son, Jesus, about my secret sins:

_____

_____

_____

_____

MY PRAYER

Lord, it's so easy to forget during day-to-day life that Jesus is coming back again and that he could come back at any time. I want to live my life in a way that won't embarrass me when he returns. Help me to confess my secret sins and let Jesus take them away.

All the world's geysers are named after "Geysir," a spouting water volcano in Iceland.

There is a hidden world beneath our feet that we don't think about too often. It's a world within the earth's thin crust, not as far below as the liquid rock we talked about yesterday. In this world are underground rivers and lakes. In some places the underground rivers form waterfalls in caves. All of this happens because the earth leaks. That's right: the ground is not as solid as it looks. Rain water dribbles through sand and porous rock (which is rock with tiny holes in it), making its way to underground lakes. These underground lakes are called aquifers, and they are the source of drinking water that we get from wells.

There are places where the aquifer pours deep down into hot rock or magma. The water boils and becomes steam. Pressure builds, and when that steaming hot water erupts back up through the ground, it's called a geyser. This comes from the Icelandic word geysir, which means "gusher." The most famous geysers are in Yellowstone National Park, which has ten thousand geysers and hot pools. These hot spots become stained by minerals and bacteria, taking on beautiful colors and strange forms. That's how these places get names like Emerald Pool, Morning Glory Pool, Firehole Falls, and Red Spouter.

Springs are created by God's own underground water filter. The cool, clear waters that come from springs start out as water on the surface. Even when this water is grungy, it becomes pure as it trickles down through the rock and soil. Then the stream breaks through the side of a cliff or pops back up out of the ground. Its voyage through the minerals and chambers in the rock turns it from dirty water into that pure, fresh drinking water those TV ads tell us about.

In biblical times an oasis created by a spring in the dry desert was as precious as a gold mine. It was carefully guarded by the herdsmen who owned it and was used to water their flocks. They had to protect the spring from other tribes that might contaminate it by using it to water their herds. The herdsmen also kept watch so that their enemies did not poison the water.

Think about what God says to you

> The Lamb [Jesus] . . . will be their Shepherd.
> He will lead them to the springs of life-giving water.
> REVELATION 7:17

The world around you is full of things that may poison and pollute your heart: friends who gossip, violent videos, music lyrics that make wrong sound right. God longs for you to keep your heart pure and clean. That's a big job! Can you do it? You bet! Just let Jesus be your Shepherd. He will lead you to springs of pure water that will make you clean on the inside as well as the outside. These springs will give you a wonderful life that will last forever.

Let's talk to God!

MY JOURNAL

Lord Jesus, I need you to lead me to springs of water that will make my heart clean from this:

_____

_____

_____

MY PRAYER

Lord, help me to stay alert and not to let my heart get polluted. Thanks for Jesus, my Shepherd, who knows the way to "springs of life-giving water."

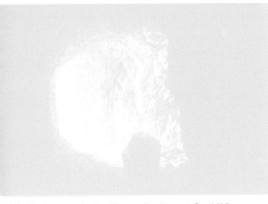

Much hidden beauty can be found in caves like this one in Death Valley, California.

The variety that God has brought to Earth comes "shinin'" through in the colors of flowers, the kinds of creatures that live here, and even in the rocks. We usually think of rocks as hard, roundish blobs, but stones come in many shapes, sizes, and colors. One strangely cool place is Goblin Valley in Utah. The desert surface has been worn away, leaving stone towers shaped like giant mushrooms. Bryce Canyon, also in Utah, looks like a magical city, with towers of colorful rock spires sculpted by the weather over the ages.

There is also a fantasy world of stone towers, turrets, bridges, and colonnades hidden in the ground. Deep inside caves, water drips from the ceiling as it makes its way from the surface down through soil

The movement of two of the earth's plates is visible in the Icelandic canyon, Thingvellir. The canyon walls, which extend out into the Atlantic Ocean floor, are spreading apart about as fast as your fingernails grow.

Even massive rocks can be folded and bent by the forces within the earth. These rocks were changed by the great pressure of two plates pushing together, not by water.

and rock. When it seeps into a cave, it brings with it minerals that have dissolved into the water from the rock. These minerals begin to build up, forming a sort of stone icicle called a *stalactite*. A good way to remember this word is that a stalactite holds *tight* to the ceiling! Below the stalactite, where the water hits, is a

149

pointed mound of minerals. This is called a *stalagmite*. Sometimes the two fuse together, forming a column from floor to ceiling.

The slowly dripping water also forms miniature trees, stone blades, and even stuff called popcorn.

In other areas water sweeps across the cave walls and roof like a curtain. In fact, the formations that are created from this are called flowstone draperies.

Within the rocks in caves we find beautiful crystals. Crystals are geometric forms that look like glass spikes, frost, boxes, or diamonds. They are made of molecules arranged in a sort of ladder, making them regular in shape. These magnificent formations are hidden deep in the darkness until the light of a miner's lamp or a cave explorer's flashlight makes them sparkle and shimmer.

Just as there are fantastic crystals and gems hidden deep in the earth's caves, there are sparkling, shining jewels in your heart—the truths that God has placed there as his gift to you. He doesn't want you to keep those gems shut up in the dark; rather, he expects you to take them out and show them to others.

Think about what God says to you

You are the light of the world—like a city on a mountain, glowing in the night for all to see. Don't hide your light under a basket! Instead, put it on a stand and let it shine for all. In the same way, let your good deeds shine out for all to see, so that everyone will praise your heavenly Father.

MATTHEW 5:14-16

How can you show your light? Here are a few ways:

This giant red rhodochrosite crystal was found in the Sweet Home Mine near Park City, Utah. (Photo courtesy Denver Museum of Natural History)

- By telling your friends about the light of God that burns in you.
- By speaking up to help your friends make good choices.
- By not going along with your friends when you know in your heart it's wrong.
- By asking yourself, *What would Jesus do?*
- By giving your time and money to people who are poor or sick.

Let's talk to God!

MY JOURNAL

God, here is one way I'm going to be a light for you:

_____

_____

_____

_____

MY PRAYER

Lord, I feel kind of shy about sharing with others all the things I know and love about you. But I know it pleases you when I do. The things I've discovered about you are treasures you have given me. Please help me to be your light in this dark world.

A Gem of a Field Trip

Go to your local natural history museum and visit the gem and mineral exhibit. Take some time to marvel at what a God we have, who cares enough to turn even simple rocks into such things of beauty!

DAY 5: GLACIERS: GOD'S POLISHING TOOL

The edges of glaciers have many colors that were created during their long journey down the mountains. (Photo courtesy Magnus Tumi Gudmundson)

Stripes of debris can be clearly seen from an airplane in this view of the Bering glacier.

Look! Up in the mountains! It's a river! It's a bulldozer! It's a conveyor belt! Actually, it's all of those things. It's a glacier.

A glacier is a river of ice that moves slowly down a mountain, carving out valleys and grinding huge boulders into sand. Glaciers begin as a field of never-melting ice and snow high in the mountains. Year after year the snows fall, and each snowfall weighs down the snow beneath it. The older snow turns to ice, which becomes thick and heavy. Finally, the ice begins to creep down the mountain like a gigantic, slow-motion river, traveling a few inches a day. The faster moving "currents" in the ice bring up rocks and pebbles from the edges and bottom of the glacier. Then the glacier carries these rocks like a conveyor belt, moving them across the ice and down the mountain. Boulders and stones beneath the glacier are rolled and polished under the great pressure of the ice. The rocky surface under the glacier becomes smoothed out and shows the scars of the rocks that the glacier dragged along beneath itself.

Glaciers change the landscape in special ways. Stripes of soil carried by the icy currents paint lines of color along the length of the great ice field, making it look like a giant, frozen zebra. Piles of rock and sand build up along the glacier's edges, leaving behind ridges called *moraines*. Where a glacier bends over a hill, cracks form. These cracks, called *crevasses,* are sometimes covered by a thin layer of snow so they are invisible. They can be deadly if an unwary climber pitches into one.

Glaciers inch down the slopes of great mountain ranges on every continent. Some of the most famous glaciers are in Alaska, Scandinavia, and the Andes mountains of South America. The largest glacier in Europe is *Vatnajökull* in Iceland.

It takes a long time to build a glacier, and it takes a long time for a glacier to change the landscape. In the same way, it takes a long time to build a strong faith in God that will help you change the world around you.

Think about what God says to you

For when your faith is tested, your endurance has a chance to grow. So let it grow, for when your endurance is fully developed, you will be strong in character and ready for anything.

JAMES 1:3-4

God's timing and sense of time is very different from yours. He chooses to have you grow up very slowly. It may seem like forever until you'll be old enough to date, get your driver's license, or move into your own apartment. In the same way, the changes in your faith may be so small and slow, you feel as if nothing is happening at all. But you can be sure that God is working in you. He has your whole lifetime to help you grow into the person of faith he wants you to be. Remember, the Christian life is not a sprint—it's a marathon. You should try to be like those glaciers, which aren't in a hurry. They just slowly and steadily march on, changing everything they touch.

Let's talk to God!

MY JOURNAL (choose one)

God, this is one area of my life that seems to change very slowly:

_____

_____

_____

_____

God, this is one thing I really enjoy about being the age I am now:

_____

_____

_____

_____

MY PRAYER

Lord, I will be patient as you help me grow into a person of faith. I want to enjoy the journey and to know you are with me along every inch of it.

ACTIVITY IDEAS FOR WEEK 9

Domino Geronimo

You can simulate an earthquake as follows: Get a shoe box and turn it upside down. On the top of the box build two houses out of dominoes and space them far apart. Stand the dominoes on end to make each side of the house, and use one for the roof. Now, be an earthquake: Tap on the box near one end. Which house suffers more damage? Why? (The closer house suffers more damage. That's because the shock waves of the earthquake are strongest at the epicenter and get weaker as they radiate outward.)

How to Make a Volcano in Your Spare Time

(Your mom will be super happy if you go outside to do this project!)

This is what you will need:

One 20-inch-square board (or cardboard covered with tinfoil or plastic)
One small baby-food jar
One pitcher to mix liquid ingredients
Dirt, sand, or plaster of paris
4 tablespoons baking soda
1/2 cup clear dishwashing liquid
1/4 cup vinegar
1/2 cup water
A few drops of red food dye

This is what you will do:

- Build a mountain of wet dirt, sand, or plaster of paris on your square board.
- Bury the baby-food jar open side up in the top of the mountain, just to the top of the jar. Don't cover the jar—this is the mouth of the volcano.
- Put the baking soda into the jar in the mountain.

- Mix the water, dishwashing liquid, vinegar, and red food dye in the pitcher.
- Pour a small amount of this mixture into the mouth of the volcano. Stir to get the "lava" to start erupting. You can repeat this experiment as often as you like!

This is what you will learn:

Gases and heat within the earth force hot lava and rock to blow out of volcanoes. In our experiment the red food dye makes the concoction look like hot lava. The baking soda and vinegar produce carbon dioxide gas. When dishwashing liquid is mixed with the vinegar, the gas creates bubbles. The gas in the mixture forces the bubbles out of the top of the small jar in the same way that lava is forced up out of the inside of a volcano.

RAINBOWS
and hurricanes

**You make the clouds your chariots;
you ride upon the wings of the wind.**

PSALM 104:3

*Tornadoes, wind,
storm clouds, and
rainbows—weather
is "happenin'!"*

The clouds turn orange at sunrise and sunset because of the way light bounces around in our atmosphere.

Weather. What do you think of when you hear that word? Clouds, rain, hail, wind, sleet, snow, tornadoes, hurricanes? Weather is what happens in the great ocean of air around us. Weather is caused by different temperatures of air meeting, mixing, and trying to become the same temperature. In an effort to even things out, our atmosphere flows in currents that move vast pools of warm air from the middle of the planet toward both cold poles. And while this is keeping the weather forecasters busy, the currents mix our air and keep the planet healthy.

Air is great stuff. Our world is loaded with it. It's made up of about four parts nitrogen and one part oxygen, with tiny amounts of carbon dioxide, argon, helium, neon, and other gases. The air around us filters out meteors, solar radiation, and some kinds of cosmic rays from deep space. It's like the earth's snowboarding helmet—God's protection for his delicate creatures down here.

It's a fact: You can't have weather without air. To see what would happen if we didn't have weather, look at a place that doesn't have any air—the moon. With no air there's no weather to move things around and nothing to even the temperatures out. If you stood on the moon without a space suit, looking into the sunlight, your face would be about as hot as boiling water, and your backside would be four hundred degrees colder—about two hundred and fifty degrees below zero! Thanks to our air here on the earth, we can wear baggy

JNCOs and Adidas high-tops instead of walking around with fishbowls on our heads.

Weather forecasters on the moon would be without a job. But on earth these people spend their whole lives studying the weather. While they still find it hard to predict the weather sometimes, the more they know, the easier it becomes for them to do their work. Weather forecasting requires a knowledge of the temperature, precipitation, wind movement, air pressure, and humidity. Wow!

In the same way, we need a lot of knowledge to be "spiritual weather forecasters!"

Think about what God says to you

You are good at reading the weather signs in the sky, but you can't read the obvious signs of the times!
MATTHEW 16:3

Jesus said the above words to the Pharisees because they wouldn't believe that he was the Messiah—the Savior whom God had promised them. They were too proud and too stubborn to see the truth, even though many had seen Jesus' miracles.

You don't need to be like the Pharisees. You can study your Bible to learn more about God. Then you'll begin to see how he is moving around you and in your life. Look around. Check to see what is happening in your church. Are there a lot of good youth activities? Look at what is happening in your school. Do you have "See You at the Pole" prayer times? after-school Bible studies? Don't hang back: Join in and be a part of whatever "spiritual weather" God is blowing your way.

Let's talk to God!

MY JOURNAL

God, this is one way I see you working, and I want to get involved:

_____

_____

_____

_____

MY PRAYER

Lord, help me to be a good spiritual weather forecaster so that I can read the signs of how you are working in my life. You talk to me through the things that are happening around me. I know you want me to join in and be part of your "spiritual weather," including the revival and renewal that you want to bring into this world.

Weather Jokes

Q: Why was the meteorologist so absent-minded?
A: His head was in the clouds.

Q: April showers bring May flowers. What do May flowers bring?
A: Pilgrims.

A thunderstorm forms over the desert.

Just like oceans of water, such as the Atlantic or Pacific, our ocean of air moves with waves and currents. As our planet turns, the sun heats the air on the daylit side, and those crazy currents set to work trying to even it all out. Within this general pattern of airflow lie many eddies and countercurrents. People have given these local winds some pretty creative names. The French Riviera is struck by the ninety-miles-per-hour gusts of the *mistral* wind. The *bora* roars down from the eastern Alps, causing plunging temperatures on the Italian coast and stirring up heavy seas in the Adriatic. The great plains of North America are warmed by the *chinook,* a wind which rolls off the Rocky Mountains and takes away the winter chill. Southern Asia has its *monsoon,* and Spain its *levante.* Whatever the name, the winds of the earth race and leap across every place—over mountains, across deserts, over the oceans, and through the deepest canyons.

We can see what the wind does to our surroundings as branches bend, clouds march overhead, and bits of grass and paper skitter across pavement. We can feel the wind in our hair and smell the new aromas it carries from far away. Sometimes we can even taste the change of the seasons as dusty leaves drift by or new flowers bud in the spring. But despite its dramatic effects, nobody has ever actually seen the wind itself. We know it is there only by inference.

We cannot see the Spirit of God either. Some have given up hope that there even is a God, simply because they cannot see him. But they aren't looking in the right places, because the Spirit moves just as the wind does. He moves in people's lives. He causes change. The Spirit of love can

Clouds mark the edge of cold air meeting warm air over the Rocky Mountains.

be felt just as surely as the warming chinook. It is no wonder that the Hebrew word used in the Bible for *wind* is the same as the word for *spirit*.

Think about what God says to you

> *Just as you can hear the wind but can't tell where it comes from or where it is going, so you can't explain how people are born of the Spirit.*
>
> JOHN 3:8

People say that seeing is believing. But Jesus wants us to know that even though we cannot see God, we can believe in him. Just as we can hear the wind and see what it does, we can see the things that God makes happen in the lives of Christians around us.

Let's talk to God!

MY JOURNAL (choose one)

God, this is one way I see your Spirit moving in my life right now:

_____

_____

_____

_____

Here is someone I am praying for:

_____

_____

_____

_____

I pray that your Spirit would blow through this person's life and help in this way:

_____

_____

_____

_____

MY PRAYER

Lord, I see your work all around me. My faith in you lets me love you and trust you even though I have never seen you. I thank you that your Spirit blows through my life and the lives of your other children. I know that my daily experiences are evidence of you and that you are always there. Praise be to God!

DAY 3: THUNDER AND LIGHTNING, HAIL AND SNOW

If it's cold enough, delicate snowflakes don't melt, even after they hit the ground. Each one of these zillions of snowflakes is different from the others!

Lightning is caused by static electricity inside clouds.

The sky darkens. Wind blows and thunder rumbles through the heavens. Soon it begins to rain, gently at first, then pounding on the roofs and filling the gutters. *Ka-POW!!* Lightning flashes through the purple clouds. It's a thunderstorm, and there's one happening right now! In fact, there are two thousand of them right now, all over the world. And the lightning from them strikes the earth one hundred times each *second!*

There's a lot going on in the clouds. The most powerful thunderstorms come from the *cumulonimbus,* the largest kind of clouds. Cumulonimbus clouds can reach up eleven miles into the sky and carry one hundred thousand tons of water. Within the clouds, tiny ice crystals rise and fall in strong winds. As they do, they cause static electricity, like the spark you get from sliding your feet on the carpet. When enough of an electrical charge builds up, a lightning bolt shoots out of the cloud. The ice crystals become bigger and heavier, until finally they begin to fall as hail or rain. Any water that falls from the clouds is called *precipitation.*

God loves to show his might and power through storms that bring us the water we need. There is no end to his creativity. He even made different ways to water the earth: mist, rain, sleet, snow, and hail. No two storms are exactly the same.

When ice crystals fall from the clouds, they often clump together into hail or melt into raindrops before they hit the ground. But if it's cold enough outside, and if the clouds are low enough, the delicate ice crystals will fall and hit the ground before they melt. This kind of precipitation is snow. Snowflakes are beautiful ice crystals, usually with six sides. Depending on the temperature they grow spikes, arms, and plates as they drift to the ground. Because each one forms at different heights and in different temperatures, no two flakes are exactly alike. Each one is unique—an individual. These natural ice crystals remind us that God is interested in the individual, in each and every person he put in this world.

Think about what God says to you

Can you shout to the clouds and make it rain? Can you make lightning appear and cause it to strike as you direct it? ... Who is wise enough to count all the clouds? Who can tilt the water jars of heaven, turning the dry dust to clumps of mud?
Job 38:34-38

Because of God's creativity, each storm is different and each snowflake is unlike any other. You, too, are different from anyone else in the world—from your fingerprints to your personality to your DNA, there is no one exactly like you! God is powerful, wise, and creative. No one but he could do all of the wondrous things described in the verses above.

Let's talk to God!

MY JOURNAL

God, this is something awesome I learned today about you:

_____

_____

_____

_____

MY PRAYER

Lord, thank you for showing me your power and creativity through the ways you water the earth. Thank you, too, for making me different from everyone else. Thank you for knowing me and caring about me just because I'm me!

DAY 4: TORNADOES AND HURRICANES

The top of this fierce thunderstorm may tower eleven miles above the ground!

How do you spell "disaster"? Try T-O-R-N-A-D-O.

Everyone knows that warm air rises. Cold air falls. When warm air rises off the plains in the spring and summer, it hits cold air that is trying to make its way down from the clouds. When these two kinds of air meet, they begin to spin within the heart of the thunderclouds. Finally, a tube of spinning air snakes down toward the earth. This funnel cloud may touch down. If it does, it becomes a tornado, the strongest wind on earth. These three-hundred-mile-per-hour winds have been known to level whole towns in minutes.

A tornado moves like a living thing. It bobs, twists, and turns unpredictably. That's how it gets its nickname. (No, not Bob. Twister.) It demolishes one house and skips another. A twister has such force that it can jab a piece of straw into a solid telephone pole and pluck a train car off its tracks. Tornadoes have also been known to pick up people and pets and gently put them back down a long way off—not unlike what happened to Dorothy and Toto in *The Wizard of Oz*. Even Disneyland doesn't offer a ride that exciting!

Another way to spell disaster is H-U-R-R-I-C-A-N-E, the most powerful storm on earth. This tropical storm forms in the ocean near the equator, where the air is warm and moist. Warm air starts to pinwheel around cooler air. Soon the winds build up to anywhere from 75 to 180 miles per hour, and the spinning hurricane grows to hundreds of miles across. Most hurricanes run out of steam before they hit land, but some crash into towns along the seacoast. The wind and rain can cause terrible destruction.

Strange, bubblelike clouds often hold hail inside and sometimes turn into tornadoes.

Does being a Christian protect you from ever being in a hurricane, tornado, or other disaster? Let's look at what God says about that.

Think about what God says to you

Disaster strikes like a cyclone, whirling the wicked away, but the godly have a lasting foundation.

PROVERBS 10:25

This verse lets us know that while scary things can happen to Christians and non-Christians alike, unbelievers do not have anything or anyone to cling to. They have no foundation—nothing strong and unchanging in their lives to help them through the hard times. But as a Christian you have Jesus.

In Matthew 7:24-25 Jesus said, "Anyone who listens to my teaching and obeys me is wise, like a person who builds a house on solid rock. Though the rain comes in torrents and the floodwaters rise and the winds beat against that house, it won't collapse, because it is built on rock." Tough things can happen to anyone, but Jesus is like a rock, a foundation that you can stand firm on when life is difficult and dangerous.

Let's talk to God!

MY JOURNAL (choose one)

This is a storm in my life that I need you to help me through:

_____

_____

_____

_____

God, this is a friend of mine who is going through a storm. Please show me how I can help:

_____

_____

_____

_____

MY PRAYER

Lord, help me not to think of you as a magic shield that will protect me from all harm, but as a friend who can keep me strong during difficult circumstances. Thank you for always being there to help me weather the storms in my life. Even if things are calm and sunny for me right now, I know there will probably be some hard times. But with you for my rock, I don't need to worry about it. You are able to get me through anything and everything.

A "way cool" double rainbow. Notice how the colors in the top rainbow are a mirror image of the ones below.

Air is colorless, but the sky—in case you hadn't noticed—is blue. It's blue because of sunlight, which has all the colors of the rainbow in it. When sunlight shines through the air, it reflects off the air molecules. Short wavelengths of light, which are blue, get through the air more easily than longer ones, which are red. But at sunset or sunrise most of the blue light is scattered before it reaches us, so the red light is what we see.

Many beautiful and mysterious sights are visible in the sky because of the way light bounces around the atmosphere. Sometimes a giant halo forms around the sun. This happens as sunlight bends when it travels through ice crystals high up in the atmosphere—the bent light forms a halo. Also fun to watch for are sun dogs. They are formed by the same process as halos, but they look like two small suns on either side of the real sun. They get their name because of their shiny tails pointing away from the sun.

Rainstorms bring another weirdly cool sight: the rainbow. As distant rain falls from the sky, sunlight shines on the raindrops and is reflected back. It is split into the spectrum—all the colors that are in light. A rainbow goes from red on the outside, to orange, yellow, green, blue, and purple.

Sun shines through rain that bursts from the clouds. Someone on the other side of this storm would see a rainbow.

Sometimes a double rainbow appears. The colors in the outer rainbow are reversed in order from the inner rainbow. For Your Information: There is no "end of the rainbow"—it's a full circle! We only see half of it because the ground gets in the way.

Ever noticed that rainbows are only seen in the morning or afternoon, but never at midday? Because of the angle at which the sunlight goes through the drops, rainbows are visible only when the sun is low and behind the viewer. The lower the sun is in the sky, the fuller and higher the arc of the rainbow will be.

The rainbow was created by God as the sign of a very special promise.

Think about what God says to you

I solemnly promise never to send another flood to kill all living creatures and destroy the earth. I have placed my rainbow in the clouds. It is the sign of my permanent promise to you and to all the earth.

GENESIS 9:11, 13

God told Noah and his family that whenever they saw a rainbow, it was to remind them of his promise never to flood the whole earth again. He said his promise wasn't just for them—it's for us also. And God has kept that promise just as he has always kept all of his promises.

God is the only perfect promise keeper. People sometimes are not able to keep their promises, sometimes they forget, and sometimes they just don't care. But God is able, he doesn't forget, and he cares. And he wants you to get into the habit of thinking carefully before you make a promise. If you keep your promises, it means you are trustworthy, like God.

Whenever you see a beautiful rainbow, remember the faithful promises of God. He has never broken a single promise, and he never will. You can trust him.

Let's talk to God!

MY JOURNAL

God, when I think about rainbows and promises, this is how I feel:

_____

_____

_____

_____

MY PRAYER

Lord, thank you for being the kind of God who never breaks a promise. Help me to remember the promises you have made in your Word. Here are some of the promises I want to thank you for:

—You will never leave me or forsake me (Deuteronomy 31:6; Matthew 28:20).
—Nothing can ever separate us (Romans 8:38-39).
—I cannot lose my salvation (John 10:27-29).
—You will always love me (Psalm 118:1-4).
—I will be with you forever in heaven (John 14:1-3; 2 Corinthians 5:1).

Bible Hunt for God's Promises

Look up these verses to fill in the blanks below:

Genesis 15:5: Promise to Abraham
Look up into the heavens and count the_____
if you can. Your _____ will be like that—too
many to count!

Exodus 19:5: Promise to the Israelites
Now if you will obey me and keep my covenant, you will be my own
special _____ from
among all the nations of the earth.

2 Samuel 7:12-13: Promise to David
When you die, I will raise up one of your _____,
and I will make his kingdom strong. . . . And I will establish the throne
of his _____ forever.

Make a Rainbow

A rainbow happens when sunlight bounces around inside raindrops.
You can simulate this by using a pan of water and a mirror. This works
best when the sun is high in the sky.

Get a pan or bowl, fill it with a few inches of water, and put the
bowl in the sunlight. Now place a small mirror under the water and
point it so that it makes the sunlight shine onto a blank wall or a
piece of white paper. What do you see? When the sunlight goes
through the water and hits the mirror, it splits up into the colors of
the spectrum, just as it does in a raindrop. On the paper or wall you
should be able to see all the colors of the rainbow from your underwater mirror.

weird and wacky
LIFE FORMS

O Lord, what a variety of things you have made! In wisdom you have made them all.

PSALM 104:24

The world is full of colorful, weird, and wonderful life forms.

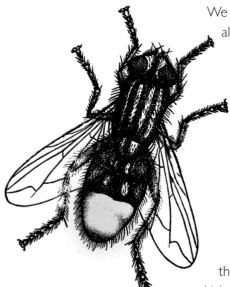

We have seen God's creative stamp in all corners of the universe—in the planets and stars, in the weather, and even in the rocks. The world is covered with life, and that life takes on all kinds of faces. There are things with horns, antlers, thorns, leaves, skin, hide, scales, feathers, spines, flowers, cones, feet, tentacles, wings, and fins.

There are many bright colors in nature, but beyond that, some plants and animals actually glow in the dark. This living light is called *bioluminescence*. Creatures flash their fashion by using two chemicals called *luciferin* and *luciferase*. These two chemicals glow when they're mixed with oxygen.

In the ocean, eight out of every ten animals are bioluminescent. Some deep-sea creatures glow all the time. Other living things, especially those on land, can turn their glow on and off. Some fish, eels, and glow worms have rows of lights. They look like a train with a headlight at the front and windows along the sides.

One of the most famous bioluminescent creatures is the lightning bug, or firefly. (Scientists call them lampyrids, but that's not as fun.) Often a blinking male firefly will fly through the air making "S" or "J" shapes to get the attention of his favorite girl firefly. The female flashes back a secret code, and they get together. This can be dangerous, because another kind of firefly has learned how to mimic those flashes. When the unwary male flies to his "mate," he may find that he's been invited to dinner—and he's the main course!

The most extreme light show put on by these lightning bugs is in Southeast Asia. Millions of fireflies gather in the trees of the tropical rain forests in Malaysia, Thailand, and the Philippines. They all flash at the same time, more than one hundred times each minute! Miles and miles of glowing, shimmering trees can be seen at night because of the radical, glowing fireflies.

Between the writing of the Old Testament and the birth of Jesus, it probably seemed very dark to those waiting for the Messiah to come and save them. During those four hundred years there was silence from God. No prophecy, no nothing. Then—suddenly—a star appeared, a baby was born, and the Light came into the world.

Think about what God says to you

He is a light to reveal God to the nations,
and he is the glory of your people Israel!
LUKE 2:32

Simeon, who spoke the above words, had waited in darkness all his life for the Messiah to come and save the people of Israel. Suddenly, there he was! Mary and Joseph had come to the temple to present baby Jesus to God. Simeon took the little baby in his arms and praised God with all his heart. He prophesied that this child had come to be a light and would help people see God, which is exactly what Jesus grew up to do. Jesus shared his light first with his disciples, then with others. Now there are lights all over the world. Are you one of those lights—a radical, glowing firefly?

Let's talk to God!

MY JOURNAL (choose one)

Jesus, this is something that your light has helped me to see about God, your Father in heaven:

_____

_____

_____

_____

I'd like to be a light too, Jesus. Help me to share the things I've learned about God with these people:

_____

_____

_____

_____

MY PRAYER

Thank you, God, for sending Jesus to earth as your Light to bring your Good News to everyone. Teach me how to pass the light on to others.

ea horse (Copyright Deborah Fugitt; City Seahorse, Inc., 930 E. Royal Lane, Suite 145; Dallas, TX 75230)

It has a head like a horse and wears a crown. It has a tail like a monkey, a pouch like a kangaroo, and thin, bony plates instead of scales. It feeds on tiny shrimp, sucking them in with a mouth tube. It would take five minutes at top speed for it to swim across your bathtub. This strange pony of the sea sure doesn't look like a fish, but it is.

The sea horse is one of God's strangest and most elegant undersea creations. Its scientific name, *Hippocampus,* means "horse caterpillar"! It has eyes that move independently, letting it see in two directions at once. It grips onto coral with its tail and waits for its food to swim by. Tiny barbs poke up from its head like a crown; in fact, this feature is called a "coronet." (A coronet is a small crown worn by people from a royal family who aren't the ruling king or queen.)

Because it is so small and slow, the sea horse's main defense against predators is camouflage. Normally it is brown or the color of sand. However, when hiding from enemies in colorful coral or sponges, it can turn a matching shade of bright yellow, green, or red.

Probably the most off-the-wall thing the sea horse has going for it is its pouch. The male has the pouch, and he is the one who actually gives birth to the babies! The male sea horse keeps the eggs in the

179

pouch as they grow. In a few weeks the pregnant male (that's right, the pregnant male!) gives birth to dozens or even hundreds of perfect, miniature sea horses. Each is about the thickness of a piece of thread. As soon as the babies are born, they swim to the nearest branch of seaweed or coral and hold on with their tails. Some of the babies hold on to the coronets on the heads of their parents, and the parents don't seem to mind a bit.

Sea horse parents like to swim around with a crown of sea horse babies on their heads. Amazing! But here's something else amazing: you are like a crown in your family too—the Bible says it's true!

Think about what God says to you

> *Grandchildren are the crowning glory of the aged.*
> PROVERBS 17:6

Isn't it exciting to know that God planned for you to be the crowning glory of your grandparents? That means you help your grandparents feel pleased with their accomplishments. They're happy to know they raised wonderful children (your parents), who in turn are raising a wonderful family that includes you! It's the mutual love, respect, and support that you and your family give to one another that brings glory to your grandparents. A loving family brings glory to God also, showing how great he is to have planned for families to live together in this way.

God created children to be a blessing not only to their grandparents but to their parents. Psalm 127:3-5 says: "Children are a gift from the Lord; they are a reward from him. Children born to a young man are like sharp arrows in a warrior's hands. How happy is the man whose quiver is full of them!"

Let's talk to God!

MY JOURNAL (choose one)

God, this is one thing I want to tell my mom and dad today that I appreciate about them:

_____

_____

_____

_____

God, this is something I will enjoy doing for my grandparents this week so they can enjoy me:

_____

_____

_____

_____

MY PRAYER

Lord, I thank you for my family. They do so many things to show that they love, respect, and support me. Help me to do the same for them.

The tropical rain forests have more life than any other land areas on Earth.

What molts, swallows with its eyeballs, and is so good at adapting that it is found all over the world? A frog, of course! Frogs are amphibians, which can live in or out of the water. When they are in the water, they breathe with their skin. When they are on land, they breathe with their lungs. Pretty handy!

Some frogs have little suction cups on their feet so they can climb trees. The average four-inch frog can jump three feet from a standstill on land, using its powerful back legs. In water, its webbed back feet make it a "jammin' " swimmer.

Frogs have a long sticky tongue that whips out and snags unwary insects. Then the frogs blink their eyeballs forcefully to push each insect down their throat. They have mucous glands that keep their skin wet and poison glands that discourage predators from eating them. They lay eggs by the hundreds in water. When the eggs hatch, they become tadpoles, which develop into more frogs.

With all this going for them, you'd think frogs would be king of the amphibians. But something has scientists worried—the frog population is declining worldwide. Some of this is probably due to loss of habitat—ponds are being drained, and trees are being cut down to make room for new communities. But there is another reason. Remember, frogs breathe with their skin as well as their lungs. Their skin absorbs water, gas, and in fact anything it touches, so they are very sensitive to environmental changes.

Frogs, which have been called "the ultimate indicator species," are being killed by pollution in our air and toxic chemicals in our waterways.

If we aren't careful, we too will absorb

Life is rich along rivers, lakes, and ponds.

the pollution in the world around us—not just physical pollution, but spiritual pollution.

Think about what God says to you

Don't copy the behavior and customs of this world, but let God transform you into a new person by changing the way you think.
ROMANS 12:2

"The behavior and customs of this world" can become very polluted. What are some toxins floating around our culture right now? Disrespect toward adults and toward authority in general, devaluing human life, drug use, and premarital sex are just a few. You have the huge challenge of living in the world but not absorbing the culture and beliefs that displease God. You need to **F**ully **R**ely **O**n **G**od—in other words, you need to F.R.O.G.! You can think of it as letting God help to transform you from an immature tadpole to a mature frog. And if you're a mature frog, you'll stay as far away as you can from anything that pollutes your body or mind. Pollution Solution: F.R.O.G.!

Let's talk to God!

MY JOURNAL

God, this is one of the behaviors I've seen in this world that I want to stay away from:

_____

_____

_____

_____

MY PRAYER

Lord, I need to fully rely on you to keep me from doing anything that would pull me away from you. I love you, and I want to stay focused on you.

DAY 4: Death by Plant

 There are many animals that are herbivores (plant eaters). But did you know there are over five hundred species of plants that are carnivores (meat eaters)? The most famous of these is the Venus's-flytrap. Small creatures that live along the coast of North and South Carolina often meet a fearsome "death by plant." Beware! That innocent-looking piece of foliage with the pretty white flowers is designed to lead insects to their doom.

A Venus's-flytrap catches its prey with its leaves, which are a marvel of engineering. The leaves are split open like an oyster shell, with spines along the open edges. Just like a mousetrap is baited with peanut butter or cheese, the Venus's-flytrap's leaves each have a yummy-looking red center. When an unwary creature bumbles in, it touches the hair-thin sensors inside the leaf, and *SNAP!* The two sides of the leaf seal together tightly around the insect.

Then the leaf acts kind of like our own stomachs do—it releases digestive juices that dissolve and digest the bug. But the whole process takes a lot longer than it does in our own stomachs. It can take from five to twenty days for a leaf to digest the bug, depending on how big the bug is, how cold the weather is, and how many times the leaf has caught prey before. The leaf can complete this process only a few times before it wears out and falls off the plant.

The diet of Venus's-flytraps includes ants, small frogs, spiders, snails, and flies. They have even been known to dine on shrimp if the tide is high! Yum!

Careless creatures that aren't alert can fall into the clutches of a Venus's-flytrap. If we don't pay attention, we can fall into a trap too—one of Satan's traps. Like a Venus's-flytrap, he makes his traps look very attractive. We need to be careful and alert, and to always watch out for him.

Think about what God says to you

> *The Spirit who lives in you is greater than the spirit who lives in the world.*
>
> *1 JOHN 4:4*

A bug caught in a Venus's-flytrap can't get out. But if we get stuck in one of Satan's traps (like getting in with the wrong crowd or developing a bad habit), we don't have to stay stuck. Through the strength of God's Spirit living in us, we have greater power than Satan and can get free from him, "the spirit who lives in the world."

Let's talk to God!

MY JOURNAL

God, this is what I will do if Satan tries to trap me into doing something wrong:

_____

_____

_____

_____

MY PRAYER

Lord, help me not to fall for Satan's tricks. Teach me that I don't need to fear him. I'm glad that you are greater than Satan and that together we can defeat him. Help me to call on you for strength to do what's right whenever I feel trapped.

Your Own Carnivorous Plant

Most plant stores carry Venus's-flytraps, and these plants are not very expensive. Here are some secrets for keeping them healthy and happy:

1. Provide a moist environment. You can plant it in a glass terrarium with a small opening, which keeps the air around the plant humid.
2. Get some sandy soil. You can probably get the right kind of soil from the plant store. If you mix it yourself, here is a good recipe:

   One part African violet soil mix
   Four parts sphagnum moss
   Five parts washed sand

3. Fill your terrarium half full of the soil and plant the flytrap.
4. Let your Venus's-flytrap have plenty of sunshine. Put it right by the window if possible.
5. If you feed your plant dead insects, be sure they are small. When you drop an insect into the leaf (use tweezers), the leaf should be able to seal up completely around it. After the leaf has completely closed, gently squeeze and massage the leaf between your fingers for a few minutes so it seems as though the insect is struggling. This will help your plant digest its food properly. You can also feed the plant small bits of lean raw meat (not hamburger—too greasy) in the same way.

Some of the strangest things on Earth live at the bottom of the sea. This painting shows the deep-sea diving submarine Alvin exploring an underwater volcano called a "black smoker." Around the volcanic vent lives a whole colony of alien-looking worms and crabs never seen before.

People have known about volcanoes for a long time. But it wasn't until scientists were able to build really radical deep-sea submarines that they discovered volcanoes at the bottom of the ocean. These volcanoes are the weirdest: stony chimneys spewing out black smoke in water so dense that its pressure would crush a car as if it were an aluminum can.

In 1979 three men dove to a great depth in the submersible Alvin, the same vessel that later explored the wreck of the Titanic. They were the first to see a "black smoker" deep-sea volcano. When they tried to take its temperature, their thermometer melted!

On later voyages scientists discovered that there was even more weirdness to come. Twelve thousand feet down in the eternal darkness of the ocean floor, where the sun never shines and nothing normal should survive, living things thrive around the volcanic vents. It's life like no place else—it's as if a spaceship dropped off an alien garden. Six-foot-long, giant tube-shaped worms with feathery pink gills sway in the ocean currents, while one-foot-long clams huddle around the hot vents. The vents that grow chimneys become convention centers for shrimp with only one eye—on their backs! This eye cannot see objects but does help them find the faint glow of the vents. Many of these creatures have no mouths. They live on energy that comes from bacteria living inside of their bodies.

Cindy Lee Van Dover is a former Alvin pilot and the only woman ever to pilot a deep-sea underwater diving vessel. She is now a professor but continues to dive in Alvin as a research scientist. She tells about the "astounding" beauty of such creatures as delicate sea stars and porcelain crabs. But she also refers to the "violent" landscape of the "black lavas that look liquid, with swirls and drapes and folds all frozen now into rock."

When people began to explore the deepest ocean, they did not expect to see things living under such great pressures. Scientists are protected by the thick walls of their deep-diving subs, but outside, the creatures have five thousand pounds of water pressing down on each inch of their bodies. Still, when researchers look out the windows, they see the rich life of the deep-sea vents. How can it be? Why are the creatures not crushed? It's simply because there is as much pressure inside the critters as there is outside of them. Their internal pressure keeps them from collapsing.

Our world is full of pressures that come at us from every direction in life. Sometimes we feel as if five thousand pounds are pressing on every inch of us. But when we ask Jesus to be our Lord, to take charge of our life, the Spirit of God comes to live inside of us. He makes our inside pressure as strong as any of life's pressures outside. God's Spirit keeps us from collapsing under the pressure of life.

Think about what God says to you

> As pressure and stress bear down on me,
> I find joy in your commands.
> PSALM 119:143

God asks so little of you—just to love and rely on him. In return, you can have a relationship with the most powerful being in the universe. He can give you the inner strength to hold up under anything life throws your way. That will give you peace and contentment and, yes, joy, even under stress. Pretty good deal!

Let's talk to God!

MY JOURNAL

God, this is a pressure I am really feeling right now:

_____

_____

_____

_____

MY PRAYER

Lord, life feels hard and heavy sometimes. I ask you to lift the weight off me, to carry my burdens whenever they come. Help me to always remember that we're in this together.

End-of-the-Week Word Search

```
B  I  O  L  U  M  I  N  E  S  C  E  N  T  X  P
W  C  H  I  M  N  E  Y  S  S  Q  R  K  L  P  O
I  A  G  L  A  N  D  S  Y  O  F  U  G  H  I  U
X  C  D  E  L  U  N  G  S  Y  J  S  P  S  K  C
Z  R  C  R  O  W  N  L  M  L  N  S  O  E  O  H
S  E  A  H  O  R  S  E  P  F  Q  E  L  I  R  S
T  U  R  V  W  B  C  X  D  E  Y  R  L  C  Z  A
V  E  N  U  S  F  L  Y  T  R  A  P  U  E  W  S
E  R  I  E  L  V  F  F  H  I  M  I  T  P  R  P
N  O  V  J  L  Q  R  A  M  F  P  N  I  S  O  I
T  V  O  N  I  O  O  P  E  R  H  S  O  T  T  N
S  I  R  E  G  L  K  F  U  L  I  W  N  X  A  E
R  B  E  C  Y  A  B  S  O  R  B  Z  A  B  D  S
P  R  C  T  D  E  F  G  C  H  I  L  D  R  E  N
T  E  H  A  I  J  K  O  L  P  A  M  Q  N  R  A
U  H  O  R  C  P  O  I  S  O  N  C  H  L  P  E
```

Find the following words:

ABSORB
AMPHIBIAN
BIOLUMINESCENT
CARNIVORE
CHILDREN
CHIMNEYS
CROWN
FIREFLY
FROG
GILLS
GLANDS
HERBIVORE

LEAF
LUNGS
NECTAR
POISON
POLLUTION
POUCH
PREDATOR
PRESSURE
SEA HORSE
SPECIES
SPINES
VENTS
VENUS's FLYTRAP

biological CLOCKS
Migrations and Seasons

There is a time for everything,
a season for every activity
under heaven.

ECCLESIASTES 3:1

God has set clocks in nature—the turn of
the stars, the change in the seasons, and
the migrations of the animals.

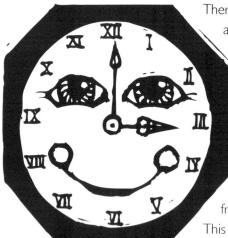

There is a rhythm to the worlds around us and a rhythm to the smallest atoms that make up these worlds. There's also a rhythm inside each of us. We all have built-in rhythms in our bodies. These rhythms are tied to the days, months, and seasons.

God has given each of us a free clock to help organize our days. This clock doesn't have hands, and it's not digital, but it's still cool. This total time-piece comes with each body, and yours is ticking inside you right now. It's telling you roughly what time it is and what should be happening in your "bod."

Is it dark out? Your body is probably slowing down for the night (even if you're a party animal). Is the sun just coming up? All systems inside your "bod" are waking up and rushing full speed toward the new day. Electrical impulses in your heart are becoming more rapid and strong. Your brain waves, however many you might have, are shifting. Your eyes are moving differently and the pores in your skin are opening. Everything in your body is saying, *Wake up!* If you don't believe these rhythms are occurring, just hop on a plane for six hours. When you get off, the night will come at a different time, and in the morning your body won't feel too great. Its rhythm will be confused.

These daily cycles are called *circadian rhythms,* and they're pretty mysterious. What makes them happen? What keeps them tuned? Are they triggered by daylight and darkness, or are they hardwired in our brains? Scientists have found clues in animals they've been checking out. Fruit flies (ever seen fruit fly?) have cell clocks sprinkled all over—in their legs, wings, and abdomens. So it seems that our biological clocks are ticking away in each of our cells. Those clocks must be pretty tiny. In fact, somebody got the brainy idea of taking skin cells from a rat and freezing them for twenty-five years (we're talkin' *patience* for this experiment!). After all that time in the freezer, those little cells still kept time.

God created time out of chaos in the moment of creation. He gave us the circadian rhythms that help us keep in touch with his world.

Think about what God says to you

This is the day the Lord has made.
We will rejoice and be glad in it.
PSALM 118:24

Do you ever feel as if there aren't enough hours in the day to get everything done, never mind to enjoy it? Do you wish there was more time to "kick back," so that school and piano lessons and soccer didn't take every second you have? Maybe you are trying to cram too much into each day. You stay up too late doing a zillion things, ignoring the message your body is sending: "Time to hang it up and catch some z's!" Then sure enough, because you didn't listen to your body's clock, you get run-down and catch a bug.

Our creator made our bodies and minds to work best when we keep to a balanced schedule of work, play, food, and sleep. Do your "bod" a favor and get nine or ten hours of sleep a night during these growing years. The time won't be wasted because you'll have more energy to "rejoice and be glad in" the day ahead.

Let's talk to God!

MY JOURNAL

God, I feel like I'm always rushing and don't have much time to relax or be with you. This is an activity I might want to give up so that I'm not so stressed:

_____

_____

_____

_____

MY PRAYER

Lord, you give me enough time each day to do what you want me to. I want to start thinking about each day as yours instead of mine.

The seasons bring a cycle of change to days and nights, to the leaves on the trees, and to the lifestyles of the small creatures and fuzzy ones that hibernate and wake up again. As autumn comes and the days grow short, perhaps the most extreme change comes in the colors of the leaves. Entire mountainsides shift from green to yellow and red. What happens?

Leaves are the food makers for trees. They have chlorophyll in them, which makes them green. The chlorophyll traps and stores the energy of sunlight for trees to use as food. This process is called *photosynthesis,* which means "made from light." In photosynthesis a tree's roots take in water and team it up with the carbon dioxide that the leaves breathe in. The chlorophyll makes sugar, which feeds the tree, and oxygen, which the tree breathes out.

When summer comes to an end, kids go back to school, the days get short and cool, and the trees stop making chlorophyll. They don't need it anymore, because they're about to take a five-month-long nap with no time out for snacks. As the green chlorophyll breaks down and fades away, the red, yellow, and orange of fall come out. The goofy thing is that those colors were always there, hidden by the green. At first the dark green holds on, outlining the veins in the leaf and making colorful puzzle patterns. But after a while, the green gives way to the bright colors of fall.

Just as the seasons cause a change in the leaves, so the Spirit of God keeps changing us, day after day.

Think about what God says to you

*As the Spirit of the Lord works within us,
we become more and more like him.*

2 CORINTHIANS 3:18

When God's Spirit gives us the desire to follow Christ, we don't instantly become beautiful, mature Christians. We are works-in-progress, leaves that may not have turned different colors yet. As our lives unfold, God grows us in directions that make us more like Christ. It's like going through different seasons, changing like the leaves on a tree.

The season you are in right now is probably very exciting but nerve-racking! Perhaps you are growing at a scary rate, and your shoe size seems to change each month. Or you might be worried that you'll never grow at all! You are busy in school learning tons about the world around you, and you are also figuring out what you believe—what is true and what is not. This season of life can be very stressful and confusing. But be patient with yourself! God is making you into the person he knows you can be. Only time will tell what beautiful colors God will bring out in you!

Let's talk to God!

MY JOURNAL (choose one)

God, I'm still pretty green in this area:

God, thank you for the beautiful colors I'm starting to see in this part of my life:

_____

_____

_____

_____

MY PRAYER

Lord, I need to trust you during this season of my life. Give me encouragement so I don't feel weird if I am growing and changing more quickly or more slowly than my friends. I know I can trust your timing.

Chlorophyll Caper

To do this activity, explain it to your mom and see if she will let you experiment on one of her house plants. If she says yes, cut two pieces of black construction paper big enough to cover one of the leaves on the plant. Now put the two pieces of paper on each side of the leaf and tape the papers together so no light can get in. Leave this "blanket" on the leaf for a week, then uncover it. What color is the leaf now? Why? Check back with Day 2, "The Seasons," for the answer.

Canada geese rest at a lake during their yearly migration.

As the seasons change, some creatures get the itch to move, and boy, do they! Birds fly south for the winter and back north to nest in the spring. Salmon swim upstream to breed, while caribou are "jammin'" to warmer pastures for food. Whales swim thousands of miles to toastier water each winter, and arctic terns fly all the way from Antarctica to northern Canada and Europe. Those terns and whales must really want a new view!

God has put into many kinds of creatures this desire to travel, or migrate. It helps them to survive hard winters and to be in safe places when it is time for their babies to arrive.

One of the most extreme migrations goes on in the Atlantic Ocean, and it's got the science gurus puzzled. Each year, on the lonely island of Ascension (also called Ponape), zillions of green sea turtles swim to shore. Their watery wanderings start in South America, thirteen hundred miles away! This is no relaxed dip in the pool; these four-hundred-pound swimmers plow through towering waves that would freak any surfer, storms that would blow the mind of the greatest sailor, and a whole lot of empty ocean. They swim for two months with no food, finally slogging onto one of Ascension Island's seven small beaches. Nobody comes up to them offering hearty meals or beverages with little umbrellas in them. The wasted turtles are on their own, and they lay eggs that will become the next generation of nature's Olympic swimmers.

The truly amazing thing is that they don't get lost. How do they find their way for thirteen hundred miles with no gas stations in sight where they can ask for road directions? How do they know this little island is even out there? (It's not like sea turtles love shuffling through world atlases.) Like many migratory animals, the sea turtles seem to have a built-in navigation system. Some scientists believe the creatures home in on the earth's magnetic fields, while others suspect the turtles can tell where to go by the ocean currents. Either way, God has placed a map inside them, glued to turtle instinct, so that each year they know where to go—even the ones who have never been there before.

Don't you wish you had a homing system to keep you from getting lost? Actually, you do!

Think about what God says to you

Your word is a lamp for my feet and a light for my path.
PSALM 119:105

As a child of God you have a built-in navigation system in the Spirit. Sure, you use your eyes and ears and arms and legs to keep from bumping into things. But there are things in life that you can't sense with your body—things of the Spirit. God has promised to guide you through the spiritual migrations that he has planned for you. He has given you the Holy Spirit to help you understand the Bible, the best road map ever made for the journey of life. God has also given you wise family and friends to help you find the things you need to know in his Word. When you feel a little lost, don't forget to ask for directions from the people he put in your life. There are no dumb questions. The only dumb thing is to not ask!

Let's talk to God!

MY JOURNAL (choose one)

These are some people who can show me what your Word says to do when I don't know which way to turn:

_____

_____

_____

_____

I need to know what the Bible says about this issue so that I won't get lost when I have to deal with it:

_____

_____

_____

_____

MY PRAYER

Lord, thanks for giving me the Bible to guide me in my life. Help me never to be too shy or too proud to ask for "road directions" when I feel as if I've lost my way.

The Road Less Traveled

To read a great book about one man's spiritual migration, check out *Dangerous Journey* by Oliver Hunkin (Eerdmans, 1985). This is a cool retelling of John Bunyan's 1676 classic, *Pilgrim's Progress*. The illustrations by Alan Parry are most excellent too.

High fashion in the forest: Built-in clocks in trees tell them when to drop their leaves for winter. As they do, the leaves take on bright colors. (Photo courtesy Bill Gerrish)

Things live at different speeds. In the jungle some plants spring up almost overnight. But in the desolate world of the arctic tundra, almost nothing grows. Living systems don't work well in dry and cold. Arctic plants come out only after the spring warms the ground, and even then they are small. At that time the tundra is covered with a spongy carpet of yellow and gray lichen. A few green sprigs of dandelions spring up here and there, but most of the color is from tiny red leaves and from white and yellow arctic flowers.

Just under these dwarf plants lies a permanently frozen layer of ground called *permafrost*. The thin blanket of living things protects this ice from melting. The layer of frozen ground holds up the entire arctic landscape above it and makes for some "way weird" scenes.

In places where the ice is covered with ponds of water, the sun warms up the H_2O and melts a tunnel into the ice. When things chill out again, ice forms domes that push up through the tunnel, making a "bizarro" hill called a *pingo*. The domes of ice are eventually covered by moss.

Another strange and stupendous arctic peculiarity looks like gigantic tiles or stop signs lying in the frozen plains. Immense polygons spread out as cracks in the soil are pushed apart by ice creeping up from below. The breaks in the ground get larger and larger each winter, until a giant-sized puzzle is laid out.

In some places the slow-growing plants of the tundra cannot protect the ice underneath—the plants may die from disease or be stomped down by hikers or ATVs (all-terrain vehicles). When the tundra blanket is gone and the permafrost foundation is exposed to the sun, watch out! The whole landscape starts to collapse into big holes in the ground where the ice used to be. A chain reaction of melting rips across the tundra, sucking the arctic scene down into the earth. This "majorly" damaged ground may take years or even centuries to heal.

Our foundation of faith is a lot like the permafrost. It must be cared for and protected. There are things in this world that can damage our faith in God, just like the ATVs tear up the tundra. What are some of these things that can hurt our faith? Scary, violent movies can make us think about the Evil One. Certain kinds of rock and rap music encourage us to be rude and disrespectful to our parents, teachers, and friends, telling us that it's OK to hurt or kill other people. Pornography in books, magazines, and on the Internet takes sex, which God designed to be something special between a husband and wife, and turns it into something twisted and ugly. Many computer games have satanic themes that take the player's mind to dark, violent places.

Think about what God says to you

Fix your thoughts on what is true and honorable and right. Think about things that are pure and lovely and admirable. Think about things that are excellent and worthy of praise.

PHILIPPIANS 4:8

What you see and hear stays in your mind forever because your brain has a permanent memory. There is no "delete" button that can get rid of the icky images once they are in there. So what's the solution? Protect your heart and mind. Don't let damaging thoughts, sounds, or images into your mind in the first place.

Let's talk to God!

MY JOURNAL (choose one)

God, these are some of the TV programs, movies, musical groups, and computer games that I know you want me to avoid:

_____

_____

_____

_____

Here are some beautiful, happy, or humorous things I can enjoy because they help me to praise you:

_____

_____

_____

_____

MY PRAYER

Lord, help me to hang a sign on the door of my heart and mind that says "No Entrance" to anything that might damage my relationship with you. When my parents say no to something I want to watch or listen to, help me to remember they have a good reason. They are doing it not because they want to ruin my life but because they love me. Thank you for everyone who helps me stay close to you.

Things live for different lengths of time on this planet. There are bristlecone pines that were saplings when the first civilizations arose in Mesopotamia, and they still watch over the desert plains of Death Valley today. Some redwood trees have been alive since two thousand years before Christ. Other plants live for only one season, churning out seeds for the next generation the following spring.

Animals have a variety of life spans too. Some tortoises live for over a century, while some insects live in the fast lane. Many butterflies live for only twenty-four hours after hatching from their chrysalis (see Week 6).

Mayflies pop out of their eggs into water, where they spend two years going through twenty transformations. (If they have a bad hair day, they don't need to worry about it. They'll have a whole new body tomorrow!) They spend another stage flying around without legs as buggy teenagers. Finally they are adults—for one day! During their "grown-uphood," they don't even have a mouth. After all, what would be the point? No time to eat!

Most mammals have about 250 million breaths in them. They live their lives out, eating and sleeping and playing and breathing. When they reach their total number of breaths, it's all over in this world! But some animals breathe rapidly, while others breathe slowly. A lumbering elephant will take his 250 million breaths over the course of about sixty years, sucking air five times a minute. A tiny hamster puffs 230 times each minute and lives for less than two years.

People take in between ten and fifteen lungs full each minute, which means that if we were like most mammals, we would be going home to heaven by the age of thirty. But God has given us humans more breaths in this world than any other mammal—actually, about three times as many.

Mayflies and butterflies probably think they live exciting lives. They certainly make the most of their short time on the earth. Redwoods have watched the march of time over hundreds of human lifetimes. What about people? How do we use our time? How *should* we use it?

Think about what God says to you

> *Teach us to make the most of our time,*
> *so that we may grow in wisdom.*
> PSALM 90:12

When you are young, it seems like forever between Thanksgiving and Christmas, and summer vacation *never* seems to come! But God doesn't want us to waste our time longing for the future. He wants us to make good use of our time so we can become wise like he is. How can we do that? Well, we can read the wise words God shares with us in the Bible. Then we can put into practice the wise teachings we've read. And we can praise God for being so great and so good, giving us so much time to do so many things!

What are you doing with the breaths God has given you?

Let's talk to God!

MY JOURNAL (choose one)

This is something wise I'm going to start doing with my time each day:

_____

_____

_____

I want to be like you, God, and take the time to do kind things for people. This is a way I will secretly surprise someone:

_____

_____

_____

_____

MY PRAYER

Lord, I want to thank you for helping me look at the way I spend my time. Show me how to do something each day especially for you. Help me to live my life as a thank-you note to you for the gifts you have given me.

GOD
is bigger than your brain

Truly, O God of Israel, our Savior, you work in strange and mysterious ways.

ISAIAH 45:15

The black hole of Cygnus X-1 pulls gas from a nearby blue supergiant star. The gases form a glowing disk around the black hole. Nobody has seen a black hole up close, but Cygnus X-1 may look like this.

A few hundred years ago an apple fell on Isaac Newton's head. It started him thinking about gravity, and eventually he figured out how things move and how gravity works. He described all this using numbers, which is pretty cool, considering most people use words (and wave their hands a lot).

Then along came *quantum physics* to really mess things up. Scientists discovered particles smaller than atoms, called *nucleons,* and even smaller particles called *quarks.* Quantum physics explains (using numbers, not words) how these tiny particles behave. All this was just fine until somebody figured out that gravity didn't add up in quantum physics, and the math in quantum physics said that gravity couldn't coexist with it. If you're sitting in a chair reading this, you know that's not true (unless you're stuck to the chair by chewing gum). Physicists knew that both gravity and quantum physics were true, so why didn't they work together?

Some brainy people discovered that gravity and quantum physics get along just fine if the universe has more than the four dimensions we are used to—height, width, depth, and time. It turns out that our universe has exactly ten dimensions. And while we operate in four dimensions, God operates in all ten of them and outside of them too.

As we saw in the first day of Week 3, God is bigger than we think. It makes sense that his creation would be too! For example, we humans like to think of time as something nice and neat that has gone on forever. Many religions say that time is and was eternal, and that the universe continually reincarnates itself. But the theory of relativity tells us that the dimension of time had a beginning. The really amazing thing is that God gave us clues about this truth in the Bible. Genesis tells us that at first there was "nothing," and then God created the universe—time is part of that universe.

Time and space had a beginning. But God had some very special plans even before the beginning of time.

Think about what God says to you

> It is God who saved us and chose us to live a holy life. He did this not because we deserved it, but because that was his plan long before the world began—to show his love and kindness to us through Christ Jesus.
>
> 2 TIMOTHY 1:9

What a mind melter: God loved you and had a plan for you before time began. Before your parents were married or thought of having children—long before your parents were even born—your heavenly Father knew you and looked forward to your arrival! Not only did God know you and love you even before time began, but he planned a way to save you from the sin and death he knew would come into the world. His plan was to send his own Son, Jesus, to die on a cross for your sins, which he did. Through Jesus you can have the gift of eternal life—a gift that God also promised to you before time began (Titus 1:2). Now that's love!

Let's talk to God!

MY JOURNAL (choose one)

God, when I think about how great you are to have made plans to love me even before time began, this is how I feel:

_____

_____

_____

_____

God, this is something I want to tell my friend about you:

_____

_____

_____

_____

MY PRAYER

Lord, you planned for me to be part of your family even before the universe was formed. That makes me feel very special and very loved!

DAY 2: Visit to a Pancake World

Pancake Diagram #1: Objects in a photograph are really just as flat as the paper they are printed on.

To help us understand dimensions, let's pretend that we are able to squish ourselves into two dimensions and visit the world of 2-D. If we look at a photo or a drawing of a house, trees, and people, it looks three-dimensional to us. But really, it's all flatter than a pancake. All of the people and objects are as thick as the paper they are printed on. (See Pancake Diagram #1.)

If we lived in 2-D Land, houses and boxes would be flat rectangles, and a water tower would be a flat circle. (See Pancake Diagram #2.) The lines of a house would leave a gap where the doorway was. If we were stuck in 2-D Land as 2-D people, all we would see would be lines. We wouldn't even be able to see shapes, because it would be as if we were stuck to paper. To really understand our world, we would have to jump off the paper into another dimension!

In the same way, God is "off the paper." He's outside of the boundaries of time and space because he's not limited by dimensions the way

Pancake Diagram #2: Three-dimensional objects squished into two dimensions. If you are stuck in 2-D Land, a box looks like a line because you cannot see the whole picture.

we are. He exists in and outside and over and through them. He's all over the place! A visit to 2-D Land helps us understand how much more God sees than we do. As 2-D people we saw only lines in our flat world. Once we jumped off the paper, we were outside of that world and could see that those lines formed squares, circles, and shapes.

The infinite God not only sees into our world, but he can touch it and move through it any way he wants to. Jesus walked on the water. But to him, as God, that water could have been solid. He was living in more than those limited properties of liquid and solid. And Jesus was able to appear to the disciples in a locked room. Impossible? Not with God, who lives and operates in all dimensions—and beyond! To God, a locked room is like a flat rectangle. Door locked? He may have just gone through the top!

It's not possible or even good to try to explain God's miracles. But thinking in more than four dimensions helps us understand how awesome our God really is.

Think about what God says to you

I am convinced that nothing can ever separate us from his love. Death can't, and life can't. The angels can't, and the demons can't. Our fears for today, our worries about tomorrow, and even the powers of hell can't keep God's love away. Whether we are high above the sky or in the deepest ocean, nothing in all creation will ever be able to separate us from the love of God that is revealed in Christ Jesus our Lord.

ROMANS 8:38-39

God is with you, loving you everywhere you go. How do you know? His Word promises you that it is true. You won't see God, even though he is always right beside you. And you may not always be aware of his presence, even though he is always there. Like the little people in 2-D Land, you can see things only from your perspective. But God sees it all. He can see just what you need, too. Amazing!

Let's talk to God!

MY JOURNAL (choose one)

God, this is the hardest part of my day, and I really need to know you are there with me in it:

_____

_____

_____

This is something that I'm having trouble understanding. Help me to see it from your point of view:

_____

_____

_____

MY PRAYER (THE WORDS OF PSALM 139:8-10)

If I go up to heaven, you are there;
if I go down to the place of the dead, you are there.

If I ride the wings of the morning,
if I dwell by the farthest oceans,

even there your hand will guide me,
and your strength will support me.

A Field Trip to 2-D Land

Take a flat piece of cardboard. Put a toy house, car, and other objects on it. Now you have a three-dimensional city—four, if you count time! Draw a line around each object. Then remove the objects so that only the lines remain on the cardboard. Now you have turned your three-dimensional town into a two-dimensional town. Notice that the house is a box. So is the car. What do other objects look like?

You can see 2-D Land from outside of its dimensions. Notice that unless part of you actually touches the cardboard, people in 2-D Land do not know you are there. Notice, too, that you can put your hand anywhere you want to, including the inside of locked rooms or the surface of things that might not be solid to a 2-D person. Can you think of some miracles that these things remind you of? God is outside of our 3-D towns, where he can see inside our cars, our houses, and even our hearts! He can also be right next to us without our knowing he is there.

God and Dimensions

For more information about God and dimensions, visit the Web site of *Reasons to Believe* at: http://www.reasons.org

DAY 3: PLACES WHERE SPACE IS WARPED

There are places in the cosmos where space is actually warped. Luckily for us, these places are far away from our own solar system.

Albert Einstein, Mr. Brain himself, figured out the theory of relativity. Part of this theory says that if something is massive enough (has enough gravity), it will bend space around itself. If it's really massive and very dense, light will be sucked into it. Then it is called a black hole.

There are several stars that are massive and dense to the extreme. The space near these stars is warped and bent toward the stars because of the strong pull of gravity. However, until recently, nobody had ever really found a black hole for sure. You can't actually see a black hole, but you can see the strange radiation it gives off as it sucks stuff into itself from the space around it. Using advanced observatories on the ground and ones like the Hubble Space Telescope in space, we now know where some black holes are, and they are scary things.

One such place is called Cygnus X-1. Like all black holes, this cosmic weirdo is a collapsed star that used to be much bigger. When it burned out its hydrogen and helium fuel, the star had a very bad day. Within a few seconds, the inner core collapsed. All of those protons and electrons that we saw in Week 5 squeezed together and became neutrons. A wave of particles called *neutrinos* rushed away from the core, ripping the outside of the star off and flinging it into space. The core of the star is now a black hole, packed together into a ball millions of times smaller than it used to be. You've heard of condensed milk? Well, this is a very condensed star!

Next door to this hungry black hole is a gigantic star called a blue supergiant. The black hole is pulling gas from the huge star into a disk around itself. The X rays from this whirling disk are what we see from our observatories. Without the blue supergiant star nearby, we might never have found the black hole of Cygnus.

But here's news: The strongest force in the universe isn't a gravity-fed black hole. It's the power of God's love!

Think about what God says to you

You are loving and kind to thousands....You are the great and powerful God, the Lord Almighty.

JEREMIAH 32:18

God has enough power and energy to love every single person in the world. His love pulls us toward him with magnetic force. In a world of violence and despair, this great power breaks through. It's a power greater than the explosion of stars or the stormy radiation of black holes. It's the only power that could create the universe from nothing, and that can turn death into life. It is the power of a love that draws us to almighty God himself, and it is capable of changing us from the very core.

Let's talk to God!

MY JOURNAL (choose one)

God, when I think about how you have the power to love all of us, it gives me the energy to love this person:

_____

_____

_____

_____

Thank you, God, that your love is so powerful that it can change me in this way:

_____

_____

_____

_____

MY PRAYER

Lord, thank you for loving me and drawing me to you. I know that your power is always available, and I want to allow you to change me in every area where I need to become more like you. Amen!

DAY 4: YESTERDAY, TODAY, AND FOREVER

We are stuck in the river of time. To us, time is a one-way ticket, a highway with everybody driving in the same direction, a rushing stream with an incredibly powerful current we can never swim against. We get one shot at each hour of each day, and then we move on.

On Day 1 of this week we learned that time and space had a beginning. On Day 2 we discovered that God is outside of physical space. The Bible tells us that he is also outside of time. The familiar words of Genesis 1:1 are a reminder that "in the beginning God created the heavens and the earth." God was already there before anything existed. God's Son, Jesus, was there too. John, in his Gospel, calls Jesus "the Word," and he says, "In the beginning the Word already existed. He was with God, and he was God" (John 1:1).

Time is not the same to God as it is to us. To God, time is like a long ribbon. We live on spots along that ribbon, but God stands apart from it. He can see where we have been and where we are going. He can see our future—in fact, he determines what it will be. All at the same instant, God sees his Son on the cross, he sees the moment we become Christians, and he sees the moment when we will meet Jesus in heaven face-to-face. It is all the same instant to him, because he is outside of time. As 2 Peter 3:8 says, "A day is like a thousand years to the Lord, and a thousand years is like a day."

Here's a mind bender: Imagine that you are God, staring at that ribbon of time. All people are on the ribbon. How would you, being outside of time, prove to those people on that ribbon that you exist? The best way is to take the ribbon and do something that only a being outside of time could do—bend it. That is exactly what God did. He told some of his prophets what would happen in seven hundred years' time. In effect, God folded the ribbon so that his prophets could touch with their mind the time of Jesus, the Messiah, seven hundred years into the future. Is your brain bent now? God is awesome!

Think about what God says to you

> This salvation was something the prophets wanted to know more about. They prophesied about this gracious salvation prepared for you, even though they had many questions as to what it all could mean. They wondered what the Spirit of Christ within them was talking about when he told them in advance about Christ's suffering and his great glory afterward. They wondered when and to whom all this would happen. They were told that these things would not happen during their lifetime, but many years later, during yours.
>
> 1 PETER 1:10-12

No other religion in the world has 100 percent accurate prophecy the way Christianity does. Only God could have helped his prophets make so many predictions about Jesus, all of which we now know came true. Here are just a few of them:

- that he would be born in Bethlehem (Micah 5:2)
- that he would be betrayed for thirty pieces of silver—not twenty-nine or thirty-one but exactly thirty (Zechariah 11:12)
- that none of his bones would be broken when he was crucified—breaking legs was standard practice in Roman crucifixion (Exodus 12:46)
- that he would die to take the blame for the sins of everyone (Isaiah 53:5-6)
- that he would be buried in a rich man's tomb (Isaiah 53:9)
- that he would be raised from the dead (Psalm 16:10)

We who were born after Christ came are more fortunate than the prophets because we can look back in time and see that God's prophecies came true. Fulfilled prophecies show us that God is outside of time. He is in control of history, and he has known the end from the very beginning.

Let's talk to God!

MY JOURNAL (choose one)

God, this is a prophecy about Jesus that blows me away:

_____

_____

_____

_____

God, knowing that you are in control of time helps me not to be so stressed out about my own schedule. Here is an area where I still feel a time crunch, though. Help me to trust you to be in control of it:

_____

_____

_____

MY PRAYER

Lord, thank you for folding time to show us your existence through prophecy. And thank you that every one of your prophecies come true. You never lie or promise things that don't happen.

The Cosmic Tape of Time

Take a long strip of paper or ribbon. Halfway through the tape, put an X and label it "me." This is the place in time when you were born. Now write down important events along the time tape. For example, before your X put a mark for when your mom and dad met. Put other happenings after your X—perhaps your first bicycle, the birth of a brother or sister, your first day of school.

Show a friend how the tape works. Wind the tape up and put your hands around it. This is how God sees time. Now open it up. We see time as a one-way trip down the tape. Notice how God can fold the tape up however he wants to, and how he can see the beginning and the end at the same time.

DAY 5: SCIENCE AND THE BIBLE

There are other religious books besides the Bible that tell about the universe around us. The Hindus, Buddhists, Mormons, Muslims, and others have their own books, which they believe were given to them by God. One of these books says that there are people living on the sun. Another book says that the stars are closer than Venus. Do these things sound true in light of what we know about the universe? Would God the Creator give a book with mistakes in it to the people he created? Many other books that people have written deny that Christ could be God, or that there could be a God who is three-in-one.

The Bible, on the other hand, revealed accurate facts about the universe long before people could prove them scientifically. The Bible told us that the earth is a ball nearly two thousand years before the Greeks and Egyptians figured out that it's round. God's Word speaks of the number of stars in the billions, while astronomer dudes said there were only about six thousand until just a few hundred years ago. The Bible is accurate and divinely inspired by the Creator!

Many people believe that the universe unfolded gradually. Some scientists say this happened automatically as a natural progression. "It's just how things work," they say. Many scientists who start out not believing in God, however, end up becoming Christians. They realize that there has to be an organizer to guide the energy of the universe. The fine-tuned universe shows them that there is a designer, a creator who is powerful.

Think about what God says to you

From the time the world was created, people have seen the earth and sky and all that God made. They can clearly see his invisible qualities—his eternal power and divine nature.

ROMANS 1:20

The Bible reminds us that we can understand the nature of God by the creation around us. If you think about some of your favorite parts of God's creation, you'll see that they tell you many things about the Creator—his power, his orderliness, his wisdom, his gentleness. . . .

You can even see God's love within his creation. The powerful God who has set the furnaces blazing in the heart of stars and balanced the forces within each atom, this stupendously powerful God treats you with care and gentleness. Instead of blowing you away when you do things you know you shouldn't, over and over again he forgives.

Science gives you a wonderful window through which to show your friends that God is real. Jesus says, "I have opened a door for you that no one can shut" (Revelation 3:8). Use this door. And always remember, as you see the geese in the sky, the rainbows in the storms, the moon and stars, and even the scum on a pond, that God is your loving creator.

Let's talk to God!

MY JOURNAL (choose one)

God, here are some things in your creation that show me how great you are:

_____

_____

_____

_____

I need your help, God, to share the wonders of your creation in a loving way with this person who thinks that science proves you don't exist:

_____

_____

_____

_____

MY PRAYER

Lord, thank you so much for pointing me to yourself through the things you have made. I see your power and creativity in the trees and mountains, thundering storms, and spinning galaxies. I see your beauty and gentleness in the shining rainbows, flowers, and delicate creatures that you care for. The way you have designed our universe, its creatures, and its people shows me how important your creation is to you. Thank you for caring about me.

Long ago God spoke many times
and in many ways to our ancestors
through the prophets. But now
in these final days, he has
spoken to us through his Son.

HEBREWS 1:1-2

There are two ways that God lets us know about himself. The first is called *general revelation*. As Paul says in Romans 1, people can see everything that God made. Through his creation God reveals what he is like, so people can't say there is no way to know God. In other words, God has made his existence clear to us by the things that he has made. Enjoy God's world. It is a signpost pointing to him and to a better life that will last forever!

God has given us another message, written not in the rocks of the earth and the stars of the sky, but in the pages of the Bible. This is called *specific revelation*. It is the gospel, or "Good News," that the creator of the universe invites us to be part of his own family by faith in his Son, Jesus.

Because of our sin, there is a gap between us and our perfect, holy, sinless creator in heaven. God has sent his Son to bridge that gap. Jesus died to take away our sins and give us a free, full life that will never end. We do not have to live by a long list of do's and don'ts. We live by trusting Jesus to save us from our sins, always knowing that it is Jesus alone who makes it possible for us to be friends with God in this life and in the next one. We live by spending time with God and by being in tune with his Spirit. The Holy Spirit gives us the energy we need to please God and a radical desire not to displease him.

Since before he created the universe, God desired that all of us would ask Jesus into our heart. Jesus came to be our Savior (to take away our sin) and Lord (to take control of our life so we don't mess it up). The Spirit of God changes our heart, and we see how much we need God. The moment Jesus comes in, we are born again and start our wonderful relationship with him.

Have you accepted God's invitation to be part of his family? If not, and if you would like to, you can say a prayer something like this:

MY PRAYER

Dear God, thank you for sending your own Son, Jesus, to die on the cross to pay for my sins. I believe that Jesus died and rose from the dead to give me eternal life. Please come into my heart right now, Jesus. I need you to be my Lord and Savior forever and ever. Amen.

Index of Bible Verses

Index of Scientific Terms

About the Authors

Michael Carroll is a freelance science journalist and space artist with a bachelor of fine arts degree from Colorado State University. Prior to free-lancing he served as a staff artist for the Reuben Fleet Science Center for ten years.

Some of the books that Michael has written are *Spinning Worlds, Volcanoes and Earthquakes,* and *Lightning and Rainbows* (Chariot/Victor Publishing). Some of the magazines for which Michael has done articles and paintings include *Astronomy, Popular Science, Smithsonian, Time,* and *Weekly Reader.* He has also created book illustrations for works by Carl Sagan, Arthur C. Clarke, Gil Morris, and Steven Lawhead, among others.

Michael has lectured at various schools and at the Denver Museum of Natural History. He has also led discipleship and home study ministries. For several years he has been an elder at Deer Creek Community Church in Littleton, Colorado.

Through this devotional, Michael is excited about the opportunity to "showcase God's spectacular universe." In addition to writing the book with his wife, he created the paintings that appear at the beginning of each week and took the photos that are not otherwise identified. The goal that he and Caroline had when they wrote this book was to combine "the things we learn from nature with the spiritual truths of the Bible."

Caroline Carroll is also self-employed as a writer, and she, too, is a graduate of Colorado State University. She has been an occupational therapist but now focuses on writing full time, along with being a full-time mom. She also enjoys painting with watercolors.

Caroline and her husband both have a strong science background and a desire to "encourage believers and unbelievers alike to learn more about the nature and power of God through the medium of science." She and Michael field-tested this book with their children and the children's friends, finding that the devotionals worked well at dinnertime and led to "spirited discussion about the subject of the day." Doing the activities with their kids' friends also gave the family an opportunity to talk with other kids about God.

Caroline has been active at Deer Creek Community Church in many different areas, serving as a Sunday school teacher, choir member, home study leader, women's Bible study coordinator, and women's ministry activity coordinator. She has also participated in many school support functions and hosted Moms in Touch prayer groups.

Two of the Carrolls' favorite places to visit in this awesome world are Iceland and Hawaii. When they are at home writing, they hang out in Littleton, Colorado, with their son, Andy, and daughter, Allie.